LINKS

WITH

THE

PAST

By the same author:

**NO PORT IN A STORM
PRISONERS OF THE SEA**

Acknowledgement:

The Author and Publisher wish to express their appreciation of the invaluable help given by Ian Chisnall.

LINKS
WITH
THE
PAST

Bob MacAlindin

DUNFERMLINE PUBLISHING SERVICES

Front cover photograph:

Greig the Starter. Andrew Greig was the Old Course Starter during the early months of the First World War. His Starter's Box was an old bathing hut.

Photograph courtesy of St Andrews Preservation Trust Museum.

Published by DUNFERMLINE PUBLISHING SERVICES
53 Garvock Terrace, Dunfermline, Fife, Scotland, KY12 7UP

© 2000 Bob MacAlindin

All rights reserved.
No part of this publication may be reproduced, stored in a retrieval system, or transmitted, in any form or by any means, electronic, mechanical, recording or otherwise without the prior permission of the Publishers.

ISBN 0-9536442-0-0

Designed by Bob MacAlindin and Roger Knapman

Printed by DUNFERMLINE PUBLISHING SERVICES

Contents

Introduction	1
The Starter	8
The Caddies	18
Winds of Change	36
The Brothers	37
The Greenkeeper	55
The Ranger	67
The Black Sheds	75
The Rabbit Trapper	77
Fore!	85
The Open Championship	87

INTRODUCTION

Of all golfing venues, none exudes the sheer character of the Old Course at St Andrews.

This almost mystical track of turf being the Home of Golf it is hardly surprising. The great Bobby Jones, having retired from the 1921 Open after taking six at the short 11th, grew to love the place so much that he once remarked: "I could take everything out of my life except my experiences at St Andrews and I would still have a rich, full life."

This, the ultimate venue for the Open Championship, will again host the event in this, the millennium year.

It has its detractors. In the modern game they ask, does the course provide a stiff enough test of golf? After all, even in St Andrews it is ranked behind the Jubilee in terms of degree of difficulty. (This would not apply during major championships when the tees retreat to lengthen the course).

Although there have been recent extensions of the Old Course which bring back into play features rendered redundant by equipment reaching ever-greater levels of efficiency, it can never compare with the likes of Carnoustie, just across St Andrews Bay, as a genuinely severe test of golf.

But the Old remains THE one they all want to play.

Part of the reason may be found in its location. For St Andrews is not just about golf.

Here in this seaside community of 14,000 souls other special ingredients combine to earn it the oft-repeated description "the best small town in the world."

With a pedigree stretching back more than 600 years the University is one of the world's oldest, many of its original buildings brushing easily aside the ravages of the weather on this exposed sector of Scotland's east coast. Competition among students to study here is fierce.

The town itself probably represents the best remaining example of a medieval city in Britain, its three main thoroughfares lancing west to east to arrive at the ruined cathedral, in its heyday second in size only to Norwich Cathedral in the British Isles.

Market Street, South Street and North Street were designed to accommodate fairs and open-air markets and retain their link with the Middle Ages in the form of the Lammas Fair, which visits the city every August.

In 1844 Lord Cockburn was moved to declare: "There exists no place in this country over which the genius of antiquity lingers more impressively."

And indeed the place does breathe history, much of it of a peculiarly barbaric nature. The initials GW and PH, worked into the footways outside the castle and at United College mark the spots where in the 16th century religious

LINKS WITH THE PAST

"heretics" George Wishart and Patrick Hamilton were burned at the stake for their beliefs.

Such was the influence wielded by St Andrews that at one stage it was virtually the capital city of Scotland. It even had its own Parliament and at a Christmas Day meeting of this body in 1645 three aristocratic survivors of the Battle of Philiphaugh in the Border country were condemned to death by guillotine. (The battle, on September 13th, saw the complete rout of the Cavaliers of the Marquis of Montrose by an army of 4,000 Covenanters, a body dedicated to uphold the Solemn League and Covenant of 1643 between England and Scotland to establish and defend Presbyterianism.)

The members, reminded of the fact that St Andrews possessed no guillotine of its own, hastily arranged for one to be borrowed from Dundee and ten days later the sentence was carried out.

Deeper into the past than any of these incidents, when the citizens of the town were obliged by law to practise archery in order to repel frequent invasions from south of the border, they would relieve the monotony by turning to golf. The King, James the Second, became so concerned that in March, 1457 he caused the Scottish Parliament to issue a decree "that golfe be utterly cryit doun."

Unfortunately locked in the memory vault of these dangerous days remains the answer to a question which must vex the serious student of the game today - were the good archers also good golfers? The techniques are not dissimilar. Just before the point of release both ball and arrow are stationary; the address is clearly important; and the wind must be allowed for. It seems reasonable to assume that if his modern counterpart is anything to go by, the 24-handicap archer must have been hard pressed to puncture even a sizeable Englishman.

Parliament's efforts to suspend play had little effect and further fulminations against the game resulted in a law passed in May, 1471 during the reign of James the Third actually prohibiting the playing of golfe. What worries bedevilled the pursuit of this innocent pastime! In 1491 James 1V endorsed the dynasty's mugging of the sport and renewed the ban upon it in yet another Act of Parliament. This solemn edict however, was effectively stymied when the King took up golfe himself!

James V played, as did his daughter, Mary, Queen of Scots who in 1567 was observed "playing golfe and pall-mall (an obsolete game in which a ball was driven by mallet along an alley and through an iron ring) in the fields beside Seton" near Edinburgh a few days after the murder of her husband.

Why do I imagine I hear as a collective whisper from the female followers of the game that most economical of inquiries: "So?"

Mary is sometimes credited, albeit indirectly, with introducing the caddie concept. While playing - which she did on a visit to St Andrews in 1567, so becoming the first lady to play golfe in the town - she was attended by cadets, corrupted eventually to caddy or caddie. Mary fell in love with St Andrews and was occasionally to be seen galloping her horse along the West Sands.

Mary's son, James VI, later to be crowned James 1st of England, was a golfer and went so far in 1618 as to ban importation of "golfe ballis" from Holland, presumably to protect the native industry.

Despite this plethora of sovereignly interest it was not until 1834, when King William 1V, also Duke of St Andrews, became patron of the St Andrews Society of Golfers (formed in 1754), that the title "Royal and Ancient" was granted to this club.

The first-ever Open was held at Prestwick in 1860 but it was not until the final two decades of the 1800s that the first genuine explosion of interest took place. The 7th volume of "Golfing Annual" (1894), edited by David S. Duncan, ran to 500 pages and contained details of officials of 634 clubs. The magazine also referred to golf as "ramifying" beyond Great Britain and Ireland with clubs known of in such unlikely parts of the world as Arabia, China and India.

The Times of India, quoted in the less exotic pages of the Fifeshire Journal of March 24th, 1870, remarked that a golf club had been formed at Bombay. Members in red coats could be seen playing on the Maidan links of six holes in the early morning between 6.30 and 8. The course was 1.5 miles long and its holes varied in length between 300 and 750 yards. On Thursday, March 17th, The Times of India said, a gold medal was played for, won by Mr W.A. Baker who was twice round in 69 strokes. The club was named The Royal Bombay Club, its motto being Vivat Scientia (Long Live Knowledge).

In July 1872 "An Old Madras Boy" - a reference to Madras College, St Andrews - wrote home from Batavia, Dutch East Indies to the effect that "despite continuous heat of 90 degrees our community is possessed of sufficient vitality to admit of the organisation of a Batavia Golf Club, having recently received from Bombay a small but appreciable supply of clubs and gutties. Of the seven enthusiasts who commenced the club five are from St Andrews, the other two being from Edinburgh."

> The puzzlement of a London correspondent whose words appeared in the Fifeshire Journal of April 17th 1879 was plain for all to see.
>
> "A number of Scotchmen," he wrote, "have left London for Jersey where, curious to relate, a golf club is to be established. Why golf should become a national game in Jersey and why Scotchmen should go there to start it are two of the mysteries of life I do not pretend to understand."

LINKS WITH THE PAST

Outside of Scotland golf remained a minor pastime until the latter half of the 19th century when with the formation of the Royal North Devon Golf Club in 1864, the game rapidly gained favour south of the border.

Even in St Andrews however, the whole concept of golf could still engender a degree of confusion. The Fifeshire Journal, during April 1877, ran a mini-series entitled "St Andrews - How It Strikes A Stranger". In the issue of April 12th an un-named visitor chanced upon a scene which he proceeded to describe as: "A number of men, many of them clearly of no mean rank, going slowly over the ground in quaint attire, and apparently thrashing the soil with pieces of slender wood."

In America it was catching on and the St Andrews Golf Club was formed in Yonkers, New York by two Scots, John Reid and Robert Lockhart. The United States Golf Association came into being in New Jersey in 1894 and the invention in 1898 of the rubber-cored golf ball by two Americans - Coburn Haskell of Cleveland and Bertram G. Work of the B. F. Goodrich Company - transformed the sport. Suddenly even elderly gentlemen found they could propel the ball good distances and there ensued a rush of new enthusiasts, including women and children.

(The new ball did not become generally available in Britain until 1902 and its effect was felt to such an extent that the Old Course had to incorporate added difficulties to cope with it. New bunkers were introduced of a size to contain little more than "one angry golfer and his club" to the right of the second, third, fourth, fifth and sixth fairways, replacing outcrops of whins).

The Haskell as it was called found itself in the legal rough when in 1905 a British court ruled that the patent lodged by the Americans was "not good". The ball, also affectionately known as The Bounding Billy, continued to gain popularity however and was always regarded as a product of American ingenuity.

This period too saw the introduction of the Ladies National Championship, played over 18 holes at St Annes-on-the-Sea in June, 1893 and won by Lady Margaret Scott. That same year the Ladies Golf Union was founded. In St Andrews ladies had been playing regularly for a number of years and what is generally accepted to have been the world's first ladies golf club was formed there in September 1867 with encouragement from the R & A. For their short course the original layout comprised 15 holes of between three and eight yards' length on ground between the Swilcan Burn and the recently-erected rocket pole. This was really a flagstaff that served as a target for practice sessions of the 25-strong Volunteer Life Brigade who fired rockets with line attached. The idea of this invention in 1807 by Captain George William Manby was to project a line across a ship in distress and thereby effect the rescue of its crew. Manby's original concept of a mortar to fire the line was superseded by rocket propulsion.

During the quarterly drill of the Life Brigade on Saturday, September 2nd, 1871 one rocket went astray and "caused considerable dismay" by landing near a party of golfers.

The pole was sited about 1,000 feet north-west of the Swilcan near the high water mark on the West Sands.

Maximum number of lady members was 100, many playing in "long skirts of broderie anglais and beflowered hats." There were gentlemen members too, up to 50 of them. This was no surprise since the person who initiated the club, D.L. Burns, was a man and its first secretary. Burns also acted as a starter from time to time.

The club was an instant hit.

"It is in every way preferable to croquet," reported the local Press "and indeed it has seriously interfered with the Archery Club, which was kept up mainly by the ladies."

Bow and arrow it seemed, were having to play second fiddle yet again to ball and club.

A local man, a Dr Macdonald, took a great interest in the new club and frequently donated prizes of jewellery to be competed for by members.

The seaside delights of this latest piece of golfing terrain - roughly where the Himalayas Putting Green is today - and of its fair occupants became the subject of a somewhat flowery letter to the Fifeshire Journal by a "D.C.S." who wrote: "The fitful cadence of the wave, in the fullness of its liquid melody, is wafted to her ear over shelving beach and tufted bank like a sigh from the heart of the midsummer sea."

It is doubtful if "D.C.S." had in mind those females who continued to use the course for a different purpose altogether - the bleaching of clothes which were often left attached to gorse and whins to dry in the sun. The Swilcan Burn itself was often busy with washerwomen and yet further domestication of the links could be witnessed on a regular basis between the burn and Granny Clark's Wynd - the beating of carpets. (Granny Clark was a Mrs Clark who ran a small inn beside the links).

Although the course was basically a putting green the ladies were also known to take a cleek onto the course. Many a competition was held and one of these took place on Tuesday May 17th, 1887 when Miss Mary Simson, playing off scratch won a handicap event. She did two sets of 15 holes in a total of 94 strokes.

It induced exactly the kind of competitive thrill which sparked in some of the more adventurous females a wish to tackle the extended game. The golfing girl however, soon found that she risked her reputation by indulging in this male-dominated activity. The raising of her club above shoulder height was certainly thought unseemly and initially her play was confined to nine holes at a time -

considered in some circles a safeguard against fainting. (This may not have been as quaint as it sounds. The form of the Victorian female was often so compressed within corsets and bodices that she could scarcely breathe).

An arch opponent of women's golf was 1886 Amateur Champion Horace Hutchinson who had won his title at St Andrews. Hutchinson's contemptuous dismissal of their participation in it still finds many an echo today among the crimson countenances illuminating bars at golf clubs throughout the land.

Although youngsters had been able to play on the ladies course, the formation in 1888 of the St Andrews Children's Golf Club completed the golfing circle in the city. The area selected for the young players was between the stone wall bordering the road at the back of the 17th green and the railway line. Hockey stick rules applied - no swinging above the elbow. Many a serious golfer laid the foundations of his game while engaged in this shortened version, often under the eagle eye of a nannie. Now everyone could play on a formal footing in that place which past Captain of St Andrews University Golf Club, R. Barclay, M. A. described as an asylum for golf maniacs.

"The very air," he went on to say "seems to be impregnated with the spirit of the game."

With the relatively sudden upsurge in the popularity of golf, the wandering mind finds itself ambushed by the thought that had there existed then an equivalent of today's meddlesome Health and Safety Executive, those randomly flying golf balls must surely have been considered far too dangerous and golf as we know it put to the sword in its infancy.

St Andrews was and is a place of pilgrimage. Only the modern version carries with him not an air of piety but a bag of clanking clubs. If St Andrews is still the candle, today's pilgrim, every bit as much as his predecessor, remains the moth. Incoming flights of such creatures originate in all corners of the world. From North, South and Central America, the Antipodes, the Far East, Europe and every clubhouse in the British Isles they home in on the Home of Golf with one thing above all others on their minds - to play the Old Course.

Its first tee, in the shadow of the Royal & Ancient clubhouse, is the most photographed in the world. And oh to be there with a driver in your hand......

I spent a single season - 1995 - as a starter on all the St Andrews courses, including the Old and while that limited spell in no manner qualifies me as an expert in that demanding occupation, it did implant the thought that a story worth telling must reside in the world that runs parallel with the players' - that inhabited by the links workers.

The golfers themselves were interesting enough. Emotional people on the whole I found, having had them in my face for an entire summer. That year I had confirmed for me an ancient truth - that while a man might be rescued from any other game, from golf never. Included in their number alas, the raconteur of that anaesthetising monologue, the blow by blow account of his round. In a game peppered by eccentricities this drone might be heard in a ties-only lounge, which sternly-applied ruling at a stroke equates that absurd article of apparel with sartorial sobriety while its wearer, under no form of restraint whatsoever, may wander at will looking like a plate of jelly and custard.

Meeting the various needs of the golfers on the courses however, was an even more fascinating army of starters, rangers, greenkeepers, caddies and maintenance men. What they saw, heard and experienced should give a different slant on the game I thought. These people after all, rubbed shoulders with Presidents and professionals, with stars of the stage and the silver screens, both large and small. They were golfers themselves very often and understood well what went on in a man's mind when he topped his drive into the Swilcan Burn at the 18th, thereby ruining a great score.

Where to start the telling of such a tale? Well, the starter seems about right. Not me of course. I had neither the time over my six months on the courses to get to know people well nor the depth of experience to garner the quality of material I was looking for.

What I required was a man with about 20 years in the job and here I was lucky enough to find the flag with pinpoint accuracy.

DAVID CHRISTIE, a St Andrews man born and bred, had not only worked as a starter for that length of time but for much of it he was exclusively the Old Course starter. No such post exists today embodied in a single individual, for the starters are moved around all over the courses.

He is the last of a unique breed.

LINKS WITH THE PAST

THE STARTER

In his home at St Andrews I found a man of 70 years of age, bad on the legs now but whose observations were presented sharply enough to have been chiselled from his mind.

Dave's recollections and thoughts suggest by accident as it were something of the celebrity status of the man in possession of the Old Course starter's job from 1975 till 1988, at which point the new system of rotating the starters was introduced. Dave finally retired in 1995.

"I hadn't been long out of the Army, in which I spent 28 years," said Dave, "latterly as a Warrant Officer in the Parachute Regiment. Once back in St Andrews I became Caddiemaster in a building behind the 18th green where the Links Trust shop now stands. After two years of doing that (1974-75) I got the chance to take over as the Old Course starter. In those days it cost a visitor £4 to play the course.

"One of the main tasks for the Old Course starter was the organisation of the ballot, Monday to Saturday. This entailed writing out the names of those golfers who did not have a pre-booked time and those lucky ones whose names were then drawn got a tee time for the following day. Names had to be in by 2.30p.m. for inclusion in the ballot for the next day. Theoretically it was possible for a golfer staying in St Andrews for say a week to enter his name every day and not get a single tee time. Luckily that hardly ever happened. I always hated to see the disappointment on the faces of those who didn't make it.

"Every now and then of course, you'd get someone trying to jump the queue. What usually happened was that a hand came into the starter's box and a sum of money would materialise before me. I always said: 'I'll give you one chance to take that away. If you remove it we'll start again and say no more about it.' They always got the message. Just as well. If I'd been offered the money a second time that person's name would never have got near the ballot. A few of these people reported that I had been aggressive or rude but that never bothered me. I was just giving it to them straight."

As the senior starter at St Andrews, Dave was responsible for some of the innovations which are still in use today. His introduction of the system of getting a round on the Old for some of those who had been unsuccessful in the ballot must have added much to the daily "take" for that course and stemmed from his ambition to see the first tee always occupied. Dave would tell them to hang around and if a likely-looking two-ball or three-ball appeared on the tee he'd advise the first waiting golfer to approach them and ask to join that game. It didn't always work but as a last-gasp method of getting that much sought after round it has done well over the years.

LINKS WITH THE PAST

Dave freely admits to a sense of nostalgia about how things were run on the links when he began there and is less than enthusiastic about some of the changes that have taken place since.

"When I started there was a Secretary and a couple of ladies. They occupied a building on the site of what is now the British Golf Museum. There were toilets there and changing rooms. The names for advance bookings were kept in a big ledger (it measured 2 feet by 18 inches) which was looked after by one of the girls. I thought she did a great job and there were never any mistakes or double bookings. There was also room for the course starters and the relief starter. I think it all worked more efficiently than it does today."

Dave has always been very conscious of the value of what he describes as "the antiquities of St Andrews." This applies as much to golf as anything else in this extraordinary town.

"It's why I feel so strongly about the erosion of the rights of the native St Andrean over the years. Did you know that until 1947 local golfers played all the courses for nothing? They had in fact already paid for their golf through the local rates. It was an inheritance which has long since been removed and I look back with some anger on the loss of that right."

Former Old Course Starter David Christie

(See The Open Championship)

As the years flowed by Dave found himself forming a close bond with some of the top names in the game. He has particularly fond memories of the American who will always be remembered as the man who "lost" the Open at St Andrews in 1970 - he of the stumpy swing, Doug Sanders.

"He was a true gent," says Dave. "Always thanked me after his round and nothing was too much trouble. Just to illustrate that, I had a cub reporter come up to me one day asking if I knew of anyone on the course he could interview.

"It just so happened that Sanders was playing. I mentioned the lad to Doug after he had played and he took him in hand and made sure he got his story and a photograph to go with it. He was that sort of a guy."

LINKS WITH THE PAST

But what about THAT putt?

Sanders had pulled a three-footer wide on the last green to hand Jack Nicklaus the play-off chance which a grateful Golden Bear took with both hands.

Commentating for BBC TV Henry Longhurst memorably described the incident: "There but for the grace of God......"

"Actually Doug did well out of that putt," said Dave. "And another thing - who else can you remember who came second in the Open?"

Nicklaus himself made a big impression on the starter.

"I had sent him some photographs," said Dave "and he wrote back. Nice fellow Jack but he didn't suffer fools gladly. You had to have something sensible to say to him or he'd just walk away.

"But for me the most significant of all the top players who came here from any part of the world was Arnold Palmer. I well remember one of those times many years ago when he played here in the Open, partnered by Bernard Gallacher. After they'd finished I was speaking to Bernard, asking him how he'd got on.

"Bernard laughed and said: 'Arnold is the hardest man in golf to play with. Whatever he does the spectators applaud him. I swear if he broke wind on the first tee they'd cheer him to the echo!' "

The man carried with him an aura, which Dave reckons, stems from the time he first appeared to play the Open in this country, in 1960.

"He was the man who opened the door, not just for the American pros to come and play here but for the home pros as well. He put the Open right back up there at the top, where it belonged.

"His view that you could not consider yourself Number One until you had won the Open seemed to hit the mark. And he conducted himself so well. A lovely man. And an honorary member of the New Club in St Andrews of course."

Nicklaus, Palmer.....but what of the last member of what used to be known as The Big Three? Gary Player.

Dave remembers him well.

"He always called me Mr Christie and I always called him Mr Player. For some reason he never seemed to do well at St Andrews but he had done the business all over the world. Tended to keep his thoughts to himself but would chat away about golf and you could talk to him too, even when he was practising. I've known people who asked him for advice at those times and he'd stop to give them a tip about putting or whatever."

Of all the home-based pros, Dave had a soft spot for Peter Oosterhuis.

"Charming chap and a great golfer. When he was playing well I thought he had the game to win anything and everything. And I told him so. Why did he not do as well as he might? May have been just a wee bit too nice. If he had had a touch of Harry Weetman in him, who knows? Weetman had great tenacity. "

LINKS WITH THE PAST

Weetman had all shown his fighting qualities in the 1953 Ryder Cup at Wentworth. Four down with six to play against Sam Snead, the British player came through to win.

Another battler was Eric Brown.

"He used to frighten the Yanks to death. In the Ryder Cup for instance he would hit the first tee with the words: 'Who's going to be second today?'"

"I got to know Eric quite well because he was a director of the locally-based Swilken Company and played their clubs. I always felt he was badly treated. For all he did for Scottish golf - and for British golf - he received no formal recognition at all. He was Captain of the Ryder Cup team don't forget and a very good one too. Never lost a Ryder Cup singles. Even when he was looking after his wife who was dying of cancer Eric would never forget his golfing duties. Got nothing at all for that degree of dedication."

Another Scot who sticks in Dave's mind is Sandy Lyle.

"He had just completed a round on the Old Course. He stood outside my starter's box and said: 'Well Dave, I turned professional just today.'"

"I wished him luck and he went on to do so well."

Of all the nationalities that filter through the starter's box on their way to the most famous first tee in golf, Dave found the Japanese of especial interest.

"I recall one Japanese fellow running down the steps in front of the R & A clubhouse onto the tee and kissing the grass. They all had a great feel for the history of golf and of St Andrews."

> Relief starter Roy MacArthur listened in disbelief as two golfers told him of their visit to an indoor driving range in Japan. As the customers hit their various shots it suddenly began to rain. No one turned a hair but they DID fetch out wet-weather gear and slip it on before continuing play. The centre created the illusion of rain by means of a sprinkler system.

Dave had golfed himself in his Army days and achieved a handicap of five. However a parachute accident put paid to playing at that level.

"I had been in freefall over France that day with my boss, a major. He said: 'Race you to the rendezvous' but the wind was really beginning to blow. When I finally opened the chute nothing felt right. It was proving almost impossible to control the drop and I couldn't brake properly. I slammed into a trench. My right shoulder was all smashed up and although I did play after that it was never the same again. You thought Doug Sanders had a short swing? I could have swung in a phone box."

The management of play on the Old Course on a minute-by-minute basis was the task of the starter and Dave had some very definite ideas on how it should be done.

"When I began in the job the time between games was eight minutes. (It had not long been extended from six minutes). That was really cutting it fine and to get any sort of rhythm to the play the ideal situation would have been to play two-balls all day, three-balls all day or four-balls all day. That idea was never adopted of course but the time lapse between teeing off was eventually extended to 10 minutes, which eased things a bit. Even then you had to take into account what I called the Geriatric Element. In any game you could get old fellows whose natural pace was slower than the rest.

"If the course becomes fouled up that's when you can get the rangers harassing people, trying to make them play at a different pace. Trying to make them run in fact. I don't approve of that at all. Nothing wrong with taking the time to smell the daisies. Some of these golfers had flown thousands of miles to play the Old Course and paid through the nose for the privilege. There's no need for that kind of aggravation. And it's no way to treat visitors to your town. These people are bound to go away with a poor impression of St Andrews."

The question of gratuities for services rendered could prove to be a sticky one for the starter.

"You had to make a judgement," said Dave. "If there was any possibility it could be construed as a bribe you refused the tip. But for the most part, people were clearly pleased with their day on the course and perhaps with the service you had given and they'd say: 'Have a drink on me,' and leave a quid or two. Sometimes it could be a lot more than that.

"Take James Garner of the Rockford Files fame. He has been a regular visitor to St Andrews and I am pleased to count him as a friend. Every time after his round he'd come over to the box and say: 'Thanks Dave. Have a night out on me with your wife. Give her all my love.' And he'd always leave £50. That was more than I was getting for wages.

"Another great friend is Glen Campbell, the singer. He plays golf in Phoenix, Arizona with Larry Clark, another friend of mine whom I met on the course at St Andrews. Larry has been coming here for 20 years. One time I was presented with a cashmere sweater by the St Andrews Woollen Mill with an inscription on it - David R. Christie, Head Starter, Old Course, St Andrews. I never wore it so I gave it to Larry. I hear it's never off his back, summer or winter. Larry and Glen play every week so it's nice to know my sweater goes with them! My late wife was a great Glen Campbell fan and every time Glen had a new tape coming out he'd make sure Sarah got a copy."

LINKS WITH THE PAST

In fact, Dave visited Larry Clark as his guest at Phoenix early in 1999. One of the highlights was a trip to the Scotsdale Golf and Country Club, where the Phoenix Open is held. Unknown to Dave, Glen Campbell, who had been filming in California, had made a point of flying to Phoenix to meet him.

"I was so pleased about that," said Dave. "He didn't have to do it."

Dave Christie (left) with Glen Campbell (centre) and Larry Clark at the Scotsdale Club.

Dave made such friends with a German couple that he counts himself one of their family.

He first met them 20 years ago when they turned up for a game on the Old Course. They had their young daughter Kirsten with them - "a beautiful wee thing," said Dave. Now he has a photograph of the same "wee girl" on her wedding day.

"Sarah and I visited them every year," said Dave. "There were five in the family, all doctors, and they lived just south of Frankfurt. Not long after we became friends the mother asked if Kirsten could spend three months with us to help her with her English. She spent a whole summer in St Andrews and we became her Scottish mum and her Scottish daddy. We went to her wedding ceremony in Germany and the family would not allow us to spend a penny. That's the kind of people they are."

Dave's scrapbook at home bristles with pictures and autographs of the rich and famous. He has been photographed with the likes of President George Bush, Henry Cooper, George C. Scott, Bob Hope, Dicky Henderson, Cliff Thorburn, Jimmy Tarbuck, etc.

"Bob Hope turned up for his game and it was tipping it down and cold with it. I didn't think he'd play but he went all the way round. Not a happy man that day though!"

Dave confesses to having been something of a stickler for protocol and is not impressed with the level of behaviour on the courses these days.

"It's definitely deteriorated," he says, "as has the standard of dress. I'd sometimes find myself having to bar people from going on the course, mainly students. Some looked like tramps. They'd turn up to play in torn jeans and grubby tee shirts. That's just not on for the home of golf."

What IS on for the home of golf, or any other course, is a tip from the starter. In Dave's case it is more a piece of local knowledge.

"Take the 18th," he said. "If you need to do well at that hole it is definitely worth considering hitting your second to the right of the hole. There is an eight-foot drop in the level of the ground on that green from right to left. And there is no doubt either that the old saying is true: a ball will always break towards the sea or towards mountains. This is especially noticeable coming home on the Jubilee Course where a straight shot will invariably break to the left."

Dave liked the quieter months best. They afforded him more time to talk with the customers.

"One fellow sticks in my mind. He had a huge beard and came from somewhere in the Canadian wastes. Turns out he was a doctor, the only one for hundreds of miles. He didn't want to play himself but he had his father with him and he DID want a game."

Dave managed to fix it for him.

"Look," said the doctor, "my one hobby is salmon fishing. I'll send you some salmon."

The starter had heard that kind of promise before.

"About two months later Sarah phoned me at work. A parcel had arrived. It was so heavy she could not get it up the stairs. When I got home I found it contained dozens of tins of salmon. The doctor had caught the fish and had them canned. He even had some smoked and labelled each tin Smoked or Unsmoked."

In another of many chats at the starter's box Dave found himself getting to know a pecan nut farmer from the United States.

"Send you some," said the farmer, who proceeded to send a sackful!

The starter on the Old Course must feel the tug of the past or he is a dead man. And he can bear witness to its effect on those today who step up to place their ball on THAT tee, hyperventilating as they do so. With his working day drawing to a close and the sun tumbling to blaze straight into the eyes of the last match as it sets out on the course, he might have good cause to reflect on the privilege of seeing The Dream Fulfilled materialise time and time again in front of his eyes. Not a bad way to end the day. And I have experienced it.

- My own sharpest memory of my spell as a starter involved four Americans who had left their pre-paid vouchers in the car. Rather than go and fetch them they opted to pay again - £260.

The Starter

I'm the starter who starts on the Old
And I've seen all there is to see
Yanks built like tanks,
Bankers that shanks,
And a windmill-like wee Japanee
On the tee

Sending them off on the Old
Down a track that is all history
Some shout at their balls
In agonised calls
Unaware they are deaf as can be
On the tee

Nothing is new on the Old
There's no wiggle that I've yet to see
The same hill of gear
Too bright to go near
With trousers that stop at the knee
On the tee

I look back at a day on the Old
On golf that has just ceased to be:
Red faces and traces
Of temper and cases
When you hear "Oh Dear Me!" openly
On the tee

(The author's prize winning entry in Fife Council Libraries Poetry Competition 1997)

LINKS WITH THE PAST

The Links Staff congregate for a group photograph in front of the R & A Clubhouse. Circa. 1964.

LINKS WITH THE PAST

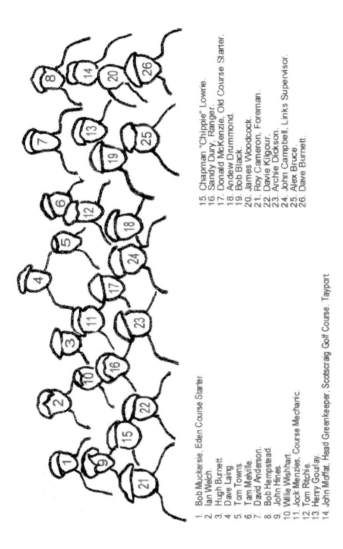

1. Bob Muckersie, Eden Course Starter.
2. Ian Welch.
3. Hugh Burnett.
4. Dave Laing.
5. Tom Towns.
6. Tam Melville.
7. David Anderson.
8. Bob Hempstead.
9. John Hines.
10. Willie Wishart.
11. Jock Menzies, Course Mechanic.
12. Tom Ritchie.
13. Henry Gourlay.
14. John Moffat, Head Greenkeeper, Scotscraig Golf Course, Tayport
15. Chapman "Chippie" Lowrie.
16. Sandy Dury, Ranger.
17. Donald McKenzie, Old Course Starter.
18. Andrew Drummond.
19. Bob Black.
20. James Woodcock.
21. Roy Cameron, Foreman.
22. Davie Kilgour.
23. Archie Dickson.
24. John Campbell, Links Supervisor.
25. Alex Bruce.
26. Dave Burnett.

THE CADDIES

The boy was 11 years old. The year was 1928. And as he stood in his short trousers at the caddie shelter at the town end of the links awaiting his first-ever client, the feet of this would-be transporter of clubs were encased in a pair of black gym shoes. No socks.

He could not have known it but during the school holidays that summer Harry McCabe was embarking upon a career which would see him outlive every caddie of his generation.

At the age of 83 he is the oldest survivor in St Andrews of that most invigorating of occupations.

As he waited that day in 1928 other boys waited too, 25 to 30 of them including his younger brother Alec. They had a better than even chance of work since golfers hired more boys than senior caddies. They were certainly cheaper. (For the record, a round over the Old Course in 1928 cost two shillings. A round on the Jubilee cost threepence).

If it rained they crowded into the caddie shelter which had recently been refurbished - and reduced in size. It was as well most of them were boys for the shed measured just 14'-0" by 7'-3".

While in the modern era at St Andrews caddies are divided into two groups - those who can offer advice and hard-won intelligence of the courses, and bag carriers whose duty entails simply that - in young Harry's day only the former category existed. Even at such a tender age the boys knew the courses well, mainly from the ball-hunting in which they all engaged and they were well qualified to navigate their golfers through the network of hazards that lay in wait.

Harry never saw a steel-shafted club in the early days.

"They were all hickory," he said "and the usual routine was for a golfer's bag of clubs to be used in the summer then consigned to some outside shed for the winter. When they took them out again in the spring the heads were all rusted up. It was one of the reasons why the clubs had to be cleaned after every round. You would take a divot to the fountain near the big flagpole at the R & A building where there were troughs for dogs to get a drink. We'd wet the divot and rub off the worst of the dirt with that, then take a piece of emery cloth and clean them completely. Finally we polished them up with a piece of rag and a tin of Brasso we always carried with us.

"Sometimes a golfer would not take a caddie but come in after his round and give you threepence or so to clean his clubs. We lads got 1/6d per round and a tip of twopence, or if he was a generous gentleman, threepence. Most of those we caddied for were R & A members or locals. One of the gentlemen I caddied for three or sometimes four times a week was Mr Eric Playfair. He was a member of the famous Playfair family, all of whom were golfers."

It was Sir Hugh Lyon Playfair who, as Provost of St Andrews between 1842 and 1861, had been at least partly responsible for transforming the town from an insanitary hole with dunghills in the street to a revitalised city with a cleaner environment and a more forward-looking attitude. Playfair, known as The Major from his Army days in the Far East, was the kind of human dynamo who attracted both anger and admiration in like volume and his reforms were by no means universally welcomed.

The boys worked the links only in summer. School got in the way for the rest of the year.

With an average time for one round of 2.5 hours it was commonplace for them to get in three rounds a day - about 12 miles, carrying clubs.

There was one R & A member however, whose appearance led to the blowing away like leaves of the untidy heap of waiting boys, even though they knew they risked the wrath of newly-appointed Caddiemaster Thomas P. Roche.

"He lived in a big house on The Scores, the road just east of the Old Course," said Harry. "A Mr Sievwright. He always wore a long black cloak and a tall black hat. But that wasn't what frightened us. It was the fact that he never gave a tip. AND you were expected to clean his clubs!"

The club-cleaning requirement was the result of a query posed to the July, 1920 meeting of the Town Council by the Caddiemaster, who wrote to clear up a point which had obviously been bothering both him and the caddies - did the caddie fee include the cleaning of clubs? Yes, was the reply from the Council, who went on to instruct the Caddiemaster to report to the police any caddie who refused to carry a bag for the prescribed fee. (This was a measure to prevent over-charging.) In February that same year the Council decided against introducing any system of formal training for caddies.

Harry caddied from 1928 till 1935 and during these years well remembers the star golfers of the day like Gene Sarazen, Henry Cotton and Bobby Jones. Harry's father Henry was also a caddie and once carried for Jones. Harry's memories of his father are hardly tinged with sentiment.

"He'd spend a lot of his time and most of his money at the 19th Hole, a pub not far from the 18th green. He got half a crown a round and a tip of maybe a shilling. He'd watch for my brother and I from the pub window and came to meet us when we finished."

"How many rounds today?" he would ask.

"Like a fool I would tell him 'three'. Alec was a bit sharper and say 'two'."

"All right - you give me half a crown, you give me a shilling," he'd say. "Tell your mother you did less than you did!"

LINKS WITH THE PAST

"Then he'd disappear into the pub again. We worked mainly for my mother. By the time dad got home he had nothing left."

Harry could not find a job after he left school and carried on caddying until, without telling his parents, he made the decision that changed his life.

"I had saved up enough from the caddying to buy a return fare on the bus to Perth. I went along to the Queen's Barracks and joined the Army. I still didn't let on to my parents until the letter of confirmation arrived. Then I had to!"

So began Harry's 25-year career in the Black Watch and the Royal Corps of Signals. But even while in the service of His Majesty, the caddying was not forgotten.

"Every time I got leave I went straight down to the links. The Caddiemaster knew that I could caddie, he knew I knew the courses so I got plenty of work during my two or three weeks at home. I was always made very welcome at the caddie shack."

When Black Watch veteran Henry John Clark left the Army he returned to the area of his native St Andrews and took up residence at Denhead, about two and a half miles from the town. To augment his income he became a caddie. Each day he walked to the golf courses, put in at least two rounds then walked home again - all uphill. Clark, whose soldierly bearing was often remarked upon, died during March 1937.

Harry was on overseas duty for most of the Second World War and seldom got home. All five McCabe brothers were on active service - four in the Black Watch, one in the Royal Navy. All but one - Alec - survived the war although John died later as a result of ill-treatment while a prisoner in Germany.

Harry's transfer to the Royal Corps of Signals came about in a most unusual way.

"They were desperately short of radio operators during the war," he said. "They commandeered signals staff from other regiments and since I was a signaller with the Black Watch, they grabbed me. Along with the other new signals personnel I was sent on a course to speed up my Morse and I ended up being able to do 37-38 words a minute."

When Harry's stint with the Corps came to its honourable conclusion he was a Warrant Officer Second Class.

Earliest known regulations for caddies at St Andrews appeared in 1771. The caddie received fourpence for going as far as the fourth hole, beyond that, sixpence.

Harry did some Walker Cup caddying at St Andrews - once for the Americans, once for the home team.

"In the 1955 event I carried for the American Don Cherry, who earned his living by crooning. Their non-playing Captain was Big Bill Campbell.

"We managed to beat the great Irish amateur Joe Carr by 5 & 4 - a fantastic achievement for Carr was one of the British team's 'bankers'. What made it worse in a way was that Cherry was playing the smaller British ball and the Americans were not supposed to be familiar with that.

"I really got to caddie for Don Cherry by accident. He had a caddie fixed up - Cowboy Herd - who complained that he wasn't getting paid enough so I got the job. And I can assure you I was VERY well paid!"

The Americans won the Cup by 10 matches to two during a cold, wet spell of weather and Campbell went round all the caddies, thanking each one personally.

It was while caddying for Britain in 1971 however, that Harry witnessed the shot that has stuck in his mind more than any other.

"I was carrying for Charlie Greene, which I had done on many other occasions," he said.

"We were looking at a shot on the last hole of a nine iron or a wedge in the tie against A. L. Miller the Third. We were just short of the road. A gale was blowing across the course. I was very surprised to see Charlie taking out an eight iron. He must have inadvertently closed the face for the ball left the club like a rocket, almost like a driver. I thought it was going to end up on The Scores. The ball was still rising when it actually struck the flag - not the stick - and fell down by the hole. Birdie three!

"Charlie never batted an eyelid. Almost as though he meant it!"

The shot could not have been more significant.

Greene and Miller had been all square on the 18th tee. Instead of going down by one hole, which would certainly have happened but for the intervention of the flag, Greene won by one hole.

The overall match ended 13-11 in the home side's favour.

> Caddies were usually golfers themselves and a match involving the caddies of 1887 took place during the afternoon of Friday, May 21st. They played for three prizes donated by a local publican. First prize: three live hens; second prize: one quarter pound of tobacco; third prize: one bottle of whisky. After the contest the caddies repaired to The Arms to toast the man who had won the hens, Bob Martin.

LINKS WITH THE PAST

An American who regularly visited St Andrews was a Mr Broadis and Harry worked for him for eight years.

"He was very particular," said Harry. "You'd caddie for him every day except Friday which seemed to be his day for doing business and on each day he'd give you a sleeve of three new Dunlop 65 balls. He'd want one on the first tee of course, and then perhaps on the 9th he would hand you the old ball and ask for a new one. Then maybe another before the end of the round.

"But by the Saturday he still knew exactly how many balls he should have in his bag and he'd count them all in the suite in Rusacks Hotel where he almost always stayed. In all the years I worked for him I think he only lost three balls on the golf courses. He was a very straight hitter."

Mr Broadis still visits St Andrews and makes a point of inviting Harry for a drink.

Harry also caddied for an Irish gentleman, Tony Gannon, for 12 years and he still turns up every year to play in the Rotary Tournament. He also contacts Harry when he comes to town.

Harry McCabe, 1999

The wife of American Ryder Cup star Fred Couples was another client - and a very fine golfer in her own right.

Harry found that the most common error made by golfers was underclubbing.

"They'd over-estimate their abilities. And when I advised them to take a club they'd never have chosen themselves they were amazed to find it took them to the heart of the green. Sometimes they almost refused to believe it. It was the caddie's job to insist his client use the right club but more and more we began to find our advice being ignored. I believe it was the dissatisfaction resulting from this that led to the introduction of bag carriers."

Some players seemed unable to come to terms with the simplest situation.

"Playing the Old Course for instance and going out against a strong wind that might add 50 to 60 yards to every hole you'd find some people persistently failing to take that into account."

Harry also found many golfers were unfamiliar with the 'right of way' on the courses.

"Incoming players always had precedence over those going out," he said. "If those coming in were being held up it meant the whole course was being held

LINKS WITH THE PAST

up and basically the 'right of way' ruling was to prevent delays to games on the back nine."

Harry played a bit himself and was a member of the St Andrews Golf Club for 15 years. He played initially with "a set of dolly mixtures" but was given a matched set by his brother-in-law who had just retired as a teaching professional. Although his play was almost always confined to weekends, he managed to achieve a handicap of 10.

But in the course of his work, Harry refused to handicap himself as some other caddies did.

"We are talking about a time when you were allowed to carry more than one bag," he said.

"I never did that. It was impossible to look after two golfers properly on the course. No way could that happen but some younger caddies did carry double. Today of course, that is not permitted."

> Town Council accounts published at the end of 1928 showed that expenditure in the sphere of caddies totalled £120, which covered repairs to the caddie shelter, the printing of tickets and the annual wage of the Caddiemaster. His salary included an extra eight shillings a week during the summer for remaining at his post all day without a break for lunch. Meals were taken to him in the shelter.

Harry recalls a colleague who lived in Glasgow but caddied in St Andrews for years.

"He was a real mystery man. He worked under an assumed name and came through every day on the bus and went home in the evening. That meant a trip each way of about three hours, although the return fare was only 9s-9d!"

Another from the early 1930s was Alex Elder, known as Niblick Nose.

No matter the distance from the hole - 100 yards, 30 yards or whatever, he would deliver the same reply to the question: 'What do I take from here?' - "Jist tak' a niblick (nine iron) and hit it!"

James Mitchell got his nickname of Deadwood Dick from a phrase he used in response to the same question put to Alex Elder and with similar disregard for distance - "Tak' a brassie and kill it!"

Carnegie Grant was another highly experienced caddie.

LINKS WITH THE PAST

"He had been in the Scots Guards," said Harry "but when he came home there was some sort of falling out with his father. From that point on, Carnegie lived rough on the links. Mind you, he did his best to keep himself clean and every day he would wash in the Swilcan Burn.

"His mother lived in North Street and she never failed to do his laundry. She and Carnegie must have had some arrangement for him to pick up the clean clothes when the father was out. And he used to keep the clothes in what became known as Carnegie's wardrobe. This was a cavity at the base of the statue to Lyon Playfair behind the 18th green of the Old Course. The 'wardrobe' was sealed by a small, square metal door."

The Lyon Playfair Statue with the "wardrobe" door

In those days there were two sets of people working the courses - summer caddies and all-year caddies. This latter group consisted largely of fishermen who caddied when they couldn't get to sea. During the war years some of them, including Harry's dad, spent more time ball-hunting than caddying. There was such a shortage of balls that it paid more.

"They would go out with dogs and pick up as many lost balls as they could and sell them to golfers. They had to contend with the occasional raid by the police but as soon as they saw those chequered caps the dogs were put on a leash and they just sat there till the officers disappeared."

Complaints about ball-hunting were common and the April 1945 meeting of the Town Council heard another such complaint directed against a particular person who was advised that "persistence in this practice will result in prosecution." At that time the standard fine for the illegal collection of golf balls was £2 but in 1950 this was raised to £5.

One of the caddies, D. Y. Cunningham, had a dog that was never on the fairway while he carried a bag. In the course of the round it would do nothing but forage in the whins for balls. When it found one it would drop it at its master's feet and would be rewarded with a biscuit. It was not unknown for Cunningham to dispense 18 biscuits per round. This level of bounty from the undergrowth prompted a ruling which banned caddies from taking dogs onto the courses.

Caddies also had to preside over the loss of many a ball during a customer's round and in no more bizarre circumstances than when a wayward drive off the 16th tee of the Old landed in a goods wagon on the train entering or leaving St Andrews.

"I often wondered where they ended up," said Harry. "Maybe down in England somewhere a railway worker pocketed a ball that had been driven all the way from St Andrews!"

One of the many Caddiemasters Harry worked with over the years was an Englishman, "Ginger" Johnson.

"He had caddied a lot in England but came to St Andrews to settle. He had nowhere to stay so my dad, whom he had met in a pub, brought him home. He stayed with us for quite a while and soon got onto the caddie list. He proved himself to be a brilliant caddie and eventually he got the Caddiemaster's job. This was pretty handy for me when I came home on leave because he'd fix me up for a whole week while other caddies were just getting a day here and a day there."

The weight of a bag of clubs began to graduate from a mere occupational hazard to a real test of endurance during the 1980s.

"They just got so heavy," said Harry. "I have carried a bag full of 14 or 15 clubs, with a spare pair of shoes inside, an umbrella and a pouch containing 30 balls. I was getting a bit elderly by that time and I found one round per day was quite enough for me. I'd often take a bag around midday, a time the other caddies tended to avoid. A midday round meant they could not get in another before close of play so most went out early."

By that time Harry was getting £20 per round, a far cry, even allowing for inflation, from the sockless days of 1928.

To one caddie - just one - was accorded the posthumous honour of having a seat placed on the Old Course as a mark of respect. Overlooking the 17th green, the seat was provided in memory of John Sorley by fellow caddies, golfers and friends. Sorley caddied for 20 years before dying in 1969 at the age of just 47.

There was never any formal attire for caddies when Harry started out but they quickly got to learn the value of wearing golf shoes.

LINKS WITH THE PAST

"On some of these sloping grassy banks in the summertime you were taking your life in your hands by wearing ordinary shoes. It was no joke to have your feet slip from under you while lugging a heavy bag."

Harry gave up caddying in 1992 but continued to work on the links where he got a morning job sand-patching.

"I thoroughly enjoyed everything I did down there. It was a good, healthy life. There were times you got a terrible soaking but it was all part of the job. I loved every day of it."

> If the level of the Swilcan Burn was low, sandbanks would appear above the surface, close to the first green and Harry remembers that golfers could occasionally play off the sand in the burn.

But who, in Harry's view, was the most knowledgeable of all the St Andrews caddies?

"Tip Anderson without a doubt!" was the immediate reply.

And as the subject of this rare compliment opened his door to me in January 1999, it was difficult not to feel a certain presence. The man standing in front of me after all, was probably the best-known caddie in the world.

Wearing Badge No. 29, Tip's father had also been a famous caddie in a career lasting 40 years beginning in the late 1920s. Old Tip, whose given name was Jim, carried for stars like Walter Hagen, Henry Cotton and the great Belgian, Flory van Donck.

A good tip for Tip's father at that time would have been about two shillings but the honourable practice of tipping caddies had nothing to do with how he got his nickname. Jim Anderson was not employed as a caddie all the time. He worked in the billiard saloon run by Fortune Jannetta near the West Port in South Street, St Andrews. He cleaned the green baize tables and re-tipped the cues - hence Tip Anderson, a label passed on to young Jim and now to HIS son, who also lives in St Andrews.

The caddie business in the early years of the century was run on a much more ad hoc basis than it is today. For the 1936 Open at Hoylake for instance,

LINKS WITH THE PAST

Young Tip Anderson at the age of 17 holding the St Andrews Boys Championship Trophy, sponsored by the St Andrews Merchants Association which he won in 1949

Photograph courtesy of St Andrews University Library

Old Tip and some of his caddie friends from St Andrews made their way to Liverpool then onto the course, hoping to land a job with one of the main contenders. Old Tip caddied for Bill Branch on that occasion.

He also worked a lot for one of the most gifted local amateurs, Andrew Dowie (See The Open Championship) and would travel with him to competitions at venues like Carnoustie to play in The Tassie or in the Scottish Amateur. Dowie, a tobacconist, would have had no problem with Old Tip's chain smoking!

"Dad was a Woodbine man," said Tip. "He never smoked anything else."

Andrew Dowie played a large part, by default as it were, in the career of Eric Brown. Brown turned professional after beating Dowie in an amateur competition. Asked why he had taken this huge step, Brown replied: "If I can beat Andrew Dowie I can beat anybody."

Old Tip had caddied for Harry McAnespie, who won the British Boys Championship at St Andrews in 1949 and was immortalised in one Press headline: <u>Chain-smoking Tip Helps Harry To Victory</u>.

Playing in that same competition, Young Tip had lost a match on the 17th green, having been seven down with eight to play.

"Had I won," said Tip, "I'd have reached the last 16 and would have played Harry McAnespie. Just as well things didn't work out that way. I don't know how we'd have got on - Old Tip against Young Tip!

"Actually we got on well on the golf courses," said Tip. "Probably better than we did at home!"

Father and son caddied in the same match perhaps half a dozen times. And when he literally began to follow in his father's footsteps, leaving his own imprints upon the same matchless turf of St Andrews, he could have had no means of knowing just how far those steps would take him.

The young Anderson's earliest introduction to the art of caddying had come courtesy of those many evenings when his father invited his golf course cronies home to his house in Boase Avenue where Tip still stays today. The lad listened and learned as the chat rumbled on far into the night.

LINKS WITH THE PAST

When Old Tip died at the age of 60 on July 1st, 1967, the family received letters of condolence from all the major golfing countries like America, Australia, South Africa etc.

"He had been looking forward to working in the Alcan Tournament in October but he never made it," said Tip.

Young Tip did not start out as a caddie, although he had dabbled in it from the age of 14.

"The first person I ever caddied for was my old schoolmaster at the Burgh School, Hugh Chalmers, in 1947. I hadn't a clue what to do. Still, I earned 1/6d I think, which took me to the pictures, got me a bag of sweets and twopence worth of chips when I came out.

Schoolmaster Hugh Chalmers, Tip's first - ever client.

"I am really a golf club maker to trade. I served my time with Tom Stewart in Argyle Street, St. Andrews near the Whey Pat pub. The firm was the last in Britain to produce hand-forged clubs. I was there for about eight years, interrupted by National Service with the Royal Artillery. I was overseas twice - over the Forth and over the Mersey!"

When he began to get seriously into caddying Tip found that his own golfing prowess was of considerable assistance.

"I was a fair player," he said. "I had been Fife Boys Champion and when I became a member of the St Andrews Golf Club as a senior I played off three. During National Service I won two Army Championships, one at Formby in Lancashire, the other at Delamere Forest, just off the Chester by-pass. It all helped. And this was true also later in my career when I had to go to other courses and you had a short time to check things out and to walk the course perhaps just twice. I found in fact, that it didn't help to do that more often."

When he ventured out of St Andrews Tip was usually en route to renew his partnership with Arnold Palmer. It was the most famous double act in golf.

"I've caddied for Mr Palmer since 1960," said Tip.

"It all began when he came to play in the Centenary Open at St Andrews. It was his first time here and he didn't have a caddie. He had just been in Ireland with Sam Snead, playing for America in what was then the Canada Cup. Wilson Staff, whose clubs Mr Palmer played, sent a wire to local professional Lawrie Auchterlonie asking him to fix him up with a good caddie. Auchterlonie first asked my father, who was not fit enough to take it on - you have to appreciate the weight of the bags used by these professionals - so I was offered the job.

"It wasn't all cut and dried. Mr Palmer said he'd wait and see what this Tip Anderson was like.

"When he turned up with his wife Winnie to play in a bounce game with Roberto de Vicenzo and Max Faulkner, the wind was blowing about 50 miles per hour. I had been in the reading room of the St Andrews Golf Club and saw him arrive. I rushed over and introduced myself.

" 'So you're Tip Anderson,' said Mr Palmer. 'OK. Grab the clubs.' "

The first time they went out together was ruined by the weather but the following day was better when Arnold shot 73 in a round with Gary Player and Frank Stranahan.

Tip Anderson (extreme left) watches Arnold Palmer in action in the 1960 Open
Photograph courtesy of St Andrews University Library.

"As luck would have it," said Tip, "We came off the course and the first person I saw was my father, who had just been in Stewart Ross's pub. My heart sank. I told him if he said anything to Mr Palmer I'd kill him! But that's exactly what he did - and introduced himself as Tip Anderson. Once all the confusion had been sorted out, Mr Palmer put a £10 note in his hand.

"Hey, that's more than I'm getting!" I said "and we all had a laugh about it but from that time onward Mr Palmer never failed to ask me how my dad was."

But what of Arnold Palmer the golfer?

LINKS WITH THE PAST

"Just brilliant," said Tip. "I had never seen anything like his long iron play. Never. A wonderful driver of the ball too. If he had a relative weakness it might have been in his wedge play. But at his peak he was such a superb putter as well. If he missed, which wasn't often, he usually knock the ball past the hole. A very aggressive putter."

That first Open in 1960 Palmer lost by one shot to Kel Nagle and if he had putted anything like his usual standard he'd surely have won. In course of the event he took nine putts more than the Australian.

Tip's experience with his new gaffer on the 17th - a par 5 at that time - illuminates the point.

"There were no yardage charts in those days," said Tip. "You eyeballed everything. During the first three rounds I told him to play a six iron to the green. He hit the putting surface every time but also took three putts every time. During the final round, held over to the Saturday following a cloudburst over the links, his drive landed in more or less the same place.

"Don't tell me it's a six iron," he said.

"Yes it is. A six iron. Sticking out a mile sir!"

"Give me a five."

"You'll land on the road."

"So I can get a five from the road can't I?"

"Yes you can. But it's still the wrong club."

Palmer took the five iron.

"Of course I knew he was trying to manufacture a shot but it did land on the road behind the green. From there he pitched up and holed out for a four. We were walking to the 18th tee when Mr Palmer said: 'Tip, you've just lost me the Open Championship! I knew you were giving me the wrong club!' We've had many a good laugh about that."

While carrying out renovations at a property in Market Street, St Andrews in 1957, the workmen of P. W. Hutton came across two notices dated 1870/71. One detailed a list of caddies - nine men and 27 boys - recommended by the R & A Caddies Committee. Each had to pay a deposit out of which any damage to the caddie shelter could be make good. Whatever sum remained from these deposits at the end of the season was matched by an equivalent sum from the R & A and the total was shared out among the caddies. So if no repairs had been carried out, the caddies doubled their money! The second notice referred to a fund out of which caddies could buy clothing. Donations from golfers and contributions from the caddies themselves serviced it.

Among a million other golfing memories about his charismatic boss, Tip recalls in vivid detail that incident at Royal Birkdale in the 1961 Open which has ever since been marked by a plaque on the course.

LINKS WITH THE PAST

"Mr Palmer had driven the ball just off the fairway on the 15th hole into waist-high grass. The ball was buried right at the bottom of this stuff - a poor result for what was really a good shot. I had my hand on the sand iron so that he could at least pitch out onto the fairway and from there take an eight iron or so and hopefully make five. That would have left him still leading the championship by two shots. I expressed this view."

"You're right Tip," he said. "At least I think you're right."

"He takes the sand iron then he comes back and we both walk onto the fairway, discussing where the next problem might be. Then he walks back and takes a six iron out of the bag. 'What are you going to do with that?' I ask. With that club he could easily have left the ball where it was, although I knew the guy was just so strong. Had very muscular forearms. He gets in there, in this jungle, to take on a shot of 150-160 yards and the next thing I know the ball is 12 feet from the pin. No one else could have done it.

"Henry Cotton was there, walking round with our game."

"Tip," he said. "That may not be the greatest golf shot I have ever seen but it was certainly the bravest. He could have blown the whole championship right there and then."

"The odd thing about the plaque they put up is that nowadays there is no sign of the long grass. It's all gone!"

Tip looks back with particular fondness on the 1962 Open at Troon.

"I had never seen golf like that. At one point he was 10 shots ahead of the field.

"But the event where I think he had to work the hardest was the Penfold PGA at Sandwich, Kent in 1975. He was five behind going into the final round and he won it by two strokes from Eamonn D'Arcy. It was blowing between 50 and 60 miles per hour. The 71 he shot that day was simply phenomenal. Only four players broke 80.

"He was a good reader of putts but on the 18th green he needed to sink a 12-footer for par. He could not seem to read this one. I had a look and suggested he aim two golf balls to the left of the hole, normal speed. I reminded him that he probably had two putts for the title but it wasn't a certainty. He took the line I gave him and rammed it right in the hole.

"That's my buddy!" said the new PGA champion.

Arnold Palmer was certainly not a one-brand club man.

"It was amazing how often he changed clubs," said Tip. "I suppose in the time I've known him he played different clubs in perhaps 30 different years. He used hundreds of putters. Once during an Open at Royal Birkdale when he wasn't doing so well he had a different putter for each round. You just can't do that and I told him so. He didn't agree with me though and after all, he WAS the boss!"

LINKS WITH THE PAST

The man from Latrobe, Pennsylvania thought so much of his St Andrews caddie that he tried year after year to persuade him to travel to America, all expenses paid, to caddie for him there. Tip was having none of it.

"I eventually had to tell him to stop asking. There was no way anyone was ever going to get me aboard an aeroplane and that was that."

One of Tip's finest hours - perhaps his finest ever - came in 1964.

"For some reason Mr Palmer decided he wasn't playing well enough to come over and compete in the Open at St Andrews. I couldn't understand it because he'd already won the Masters that year. But his great friend Tony Lema was coming and Mr Palmer told him to contact me. He arrived in time for one practice round plus a wee stroll about. I told him it wasn't enough because conditions can change so dramatically from day to day."

"But Arnold says...."

"Arnold is not caddying for you," I reminded him.

"However, he had borrowed a putter from Mr Palmer and he putted just great throughout the tournament. In fact he played wonderful golf. The man had every shot in the bag. Each time I told him to hit the ball into a certain place he did exactly that on every occasion bar one. He was so accurate that in the entire 72 holes he was never in a bunker. Probably that had never been done before."

Lema was full of praise for the caddie. He reckoned his success was 49% down to him, 51% to Tip Anderson.

Tip thought that was a touch over the top but the dedication to detail of the local man was indeed legendary.

"You have to be observant and thorough. You have to know the rules of golf and frankly you don't find that to the same extent among caddies today. Even some of the players are pretty vague."

One instance on the tee as Lema was about to set out on his first round demonstrates the value of the clued-up caddie.

"I noticed his sand iron had substantial punch marks. I thought the holes might be a bit deep and possibly they would infringe the rules. I had it checked out with the R & A through Brigadier Crawford who cleared the club for play.

"Good thinking Tip," said Tony Lema. "But we won't be going in any bunkers anyway."

"How right he was!"

Tip spoke almost in awe of the run Lema had during the third round.

"At one time we had been seven in front but Jack Nicklaus was on the 11th and had cut the lead to just one. From the sixth Mr Lema went 3, 3, 3, 3, 3, 3, 3. We were playing two rounds a day then, on the Friday, and when the lead fell to one again in Round Four Tony did almost exactly the same run and we won by five shots in the end.

"On the final hole he was about to play a wedge when I told him: 'Hold it! Show these locals at St Andrews that you can play a pitch and run as well as they can.' I gave him a seven iron and told him where to land it, up into the right corner of the green. He pitched it within a foot of where I told him to and it came to rest about four feet from the stick."

In later years Arnold Palmer was asked if he had ever won the Open at St Andrews.

"No," he said, "but I feel almost as though I had. After all, Tony Lema won with my putter AND my caddie!"

Lema's nickname of Champagne Tony derived from a habit he had got into of plying the Press with champagne after every victory. It was a practice which was to rebound on Tip Anderson in a positively painful way.

"Mr Lema had given me more money than usual after the Open. He said he had never given a caddie such a sum before but he figured I had earned it. He also gave me something extra so that I could buy some champagne. It didn't suit me at all and it burst an ulcer in my stomach. I spent 10 days in hospital."

For the caddie, practice days for a major championship could be a lot more taxing than the event itself.

"I've often carried Mr Palmer's bag during practice when it had two full sets of clubs in it. 30 clubs. You had to be pretty fit for that and remember, it was common to play two practice rounds in a day. When it came to the championship proper, with just 14 clubs in the bag, it was a piece of cake."

Tip's main tip to the average golfer at St Andrews is to take a putter for anything within 20 yards of the green. He reckons it could save the player up to four strokes a round.

"Arnold Palmer would do exactly that. And that's another thing about caddying - you have to know your golfer. I found quite quickly that I could apply a simple rule of thumb to Mr Palmer's game. He hit the ball about two clubs longer than I could so if I would have played a five iron I'd give him a seven and so on. It worked pretty well."

And the most dangerous bunker on the Old Course?

"Whatever you do, try to avoid the Hill Bunker to the left of the short 11th. If you get in there, look out! All the bunkers are tough to negotiate but I would say that's the hardest."

One of Tip's most nightmarish experiences came in the Seniors Championship at Turnberry a few years back, caddying again for Arnold Palmer.

"The weather was unbelievable. It just never stopped raining. They were sweeping water off the greens in front of us as we played. It took us six and a half hours to complete one round. Arnold came third on that occasion. Mrs Palmer must have come out with a dozen towels to different parts of the course."

Tip worked for Palmer in many a Ryder Cup.

"He and his usual partner, Billy Casper, were unbeatable. Arnold has won more Ryder Cup points than any other golfer - 22 - although he did lose quite badly to Peter Oosterhuis at Muirfield."

LINKS WITH THE PAST

Tip caddied for several R & A members including Joe Carr and his son Roddy and for Rodney Foster from Bradford. Tip will still take a bag at St Andrews, where he has been caddying for 51 years.

> During December, 1971, Provost David Niven of St Andrews, while handling his ceremonial robe, felt something between the lining and the ermine of the garment. It was a tee peg. "How it got there I do not know," he said "but I think it should remain where it is a further link between St Andrews and golf."

"I'm often asked how long it took me to learn the courses here. I can't answer the question. You see, I'm still learning."

In the early years the caddies got a ticket from the Caddiemaster at the beginning of each round and were paid when it was returned. The rates changed with the passage of time but Tip remembers he used to be paid "around an old dollar - about five bob."

He'd usually caddie twice a day, five days a week and often he would play at weekends in medal competitions and the like.

Tip had more time for the caddies of former days.

"They WERE a good bunch. You'd help one another. I recall an incident when I was at Southport to caddie for Mr Palmer. Dave Stockton was playing and had asked me to work for him. Though I didn't know it then, Mr Palmer had decided to cancel and I put Mr Stockton onto Charlie Mackie, another St Andrews caddie who had worked for people like Gary Player and Frank Stranahan. When Mr Palmer withdrew that night I was left without a bag. I had a word with Charlie, who insisted I take up the Stockton offer.

"I explained about Charlie to Mr Stockton who promised to see him all right and I saw him too, to make sure he wouldn't go empty-handed. In the event, Charlie got another bag anyway."

Tip caddied for some of the country's best-known lady golfers, including Belle Robertson, who won the Scottish Ladies Championship a record seven times and who had been Captain of the Curtis Cup team.

"Ladies tend to be better listeners than men," said Tip. "If I gave Belle a piece of advice for example, she always followed it. Belle still keeps in touch."

From the world of showbiz, Bruce Forsyth is a regular client and Sean Connery never passes without a word or two, or a drink or two!

Tip is not a fan of the 4.5 hour plus round of golf.

"At one time if you took three hours for 18 holes you got a rap on the knuckles. Now there are so many people playing that you do well to get round in four hours. I can't be bothered with those people who line up 18-inch putts. I just tell them to step up and hit it. Americans can be really slow and I never like to have the rangers on my back, which is what happens if you fall behind.

"I still like the Americans perhaps better than any of the other nationalities who come to play St Andrews. They have a great sense of the history of the place and of course as soon as you mention you caddie for Arnold Palmer they are rather impressed!"

Tip was too unwell to caddie during the 1995 Open at St Andrews but Palmer left a fee for him anyway.

Tip remembers what may have been the longest drive hit by Palmer, at St Andrews in 1961 during a televised exhibition match with Gary Player.

"He drove into the Benty Bunker on the 14th. I never thought he could reach it, otherwise I'd have given him a three wood. There might have been a touch of following wind but that bunker is more than 400 yards from the tee."

Unlike that drive, which came to rest in sand after its epic flight, the Palmer-Anderson saga continues serenely on. Though the rapport remains it is a more fitful arrangement than in former times when the American bestrode the world of golf like a Colossus but whenever he comes to St Andrews to take part in some local event, the partnership picks up where it left off.

And how would Tip sum up his career?

"Simple. When you have caddied for Arnold Palmer, what else is there?"

Arnold Palmer with Tip crossing the Swilcan after the drive from the 18th tee during the first ever televised match at St Andrews in July 1961 between Palmer and Gary Player. Palmer shot 70, Player 75.

Photograph courtesy of St Andrews University Library.

LINKS WITH THE PAST

WINDS OF CHANGE

In the space of the lifetimes of those who feature in this book, the management of golf at St Andrews has undergone some startling changes.

The age-old arrangement, whose beginnings can be traced to the 1890s, placed responsibility for the Old and New courses firmly with the Royal and Ancient Golf Club while the other two main courses, the Jubilee, formed in 1897 and the Eden (1914), were looked after by St Andrews Town Council.

Both organisations had their own staff on the courses.

The system survived two world wars and many upheavals as the popularity of the game waxed and waned and as both technologies and attitudes shifted ever further along the road to turning golf into the most popular sport on earth capable of being played by a single individual.

The first principal alteration in the wake of the Second World War came in May, 1953 when a joint maintenance pact was put in place, resulting in all of the R & A's starters and greenkeepers being transferred to the Town Council's Links Department.

However, bigger changes yet were in prospect.

Ownership of the links land being vested in the local authority, it was a matter of the gravest concern to local golfers when it became apparent that the Town Council was about to be rendered redundant as a shake-up of the country's local authorities loomed large on the horizon.

During 1974, one year in advance of the change which would see the Town Council replaced by the much larger North-East Fife District Council, an Act of Parliament was passed allowing for the formation of a new body to manage the courses, St Andrews Links Trust. In conjunction with the Links Management Committee, the Trust would be responsible for the maintenance of the links "as a public park and place of public resort and recreation for the residents of St Andrews and others resorting thereto."

The Links Trust survived a further major spasm in 1996 as local authorities were piloted into ever-deeper canyons of inefficiency with yet more centralisation. (Have you ever succeeded in getting anyone from a large local authority to return a phone call?)

The new owners of the links, The Fife Council, were now further away than ever from St Andrews, based in Glenrothes 20 miles away.

So, for the time being, things remain. The Fife Council, to their credit, have pledged not to interfere with the 1974 Act. It is devoutly to be hoped they will continue to ride this beam of common sense.

LINKS WITH THE PAST

THE BROTHERS

When 14-year-old Robert Ritchie joined the staff at St Andrews links straight from the Burgh School in 1942 the Second World War was at its height. With most of the menfolk fighting on foreign fields, including his brother who was in the Black Watch, Robert found himself a boy among older men. One of these was Andrew Nicol, his uncle, a member of the local Dad's Army, which had its guardhouse in the gents waiting room at the Bruce Embankment.

Young Ritchie started off as an apprentice greenkeeper on the Eden and Jubilee courses at the princely remuneration of £2-10s a week. He and his workmates, who numbered about 14, included Dave "Popeye" Grieve, who only had one eye. They operated from a yellow pine shed between the 1st and 17th greens of the Jubilee, which had been bought in 1939 for £85 by St Andrews Town Council.

"What we had to work with in those days were mainly hand tools. But our squad also had 20-inch Ransome petrol mowers and Andrew Drummond - who was to become the under foreman - and I, cut the greens with those. There were also smaller Ransomes for cutting tees. We'd usually cut greens in the mornings, tees in the afternoons. In winter we were often sent out to hand-weed the greens, even if it was snowing. You could never get warm doing that job."

> The rates for playing the four courses were: Old, 2/6d; New, 1/6d; Eden, 1/6d; Jubilee, 6d. These rates remained unaltered for the duration of the war.

Sometimes they'd also spread a worm killer on the greens - usually powder lead arsenate - to try to cut down on the number of worm casts, a major problem for the workmen. Robert recollects an experiment to get rid of the worms, conducted on the 5th, 6th, 11th, 12th and 13th greens of the Eden Course.

"The fire engine was driven out to the Eden estuary one Sunday in November and it sprayed these greens with salt water. That did the trick. It brought the worms to the surface and we just swept them away with brooms. The greens appeared yellow for a while but some fertiliser soon put that right. It was very noticeable that after the salt water treatment the grass went very wiry. The greens remained in that very hard-wearing condition until about June or July."

LINKS WITH THE PAST

The Eden and Jubilee men had two Pattison Metropolitan golf course tractors at their disposal for towing mowers to cut the fairways but one disappeared for most of the war. It had been commandeered to tow a grass mower at a local airfield. These tractors had slim rubber-tyred front wheels and wide, unshod metal wheels at the back. These were indented with a number of holes into which spikes could be inserted to effect a crude type of soil aeration.

The Town Council's Pattison was allowed 12 miles per week of road travel before a licence was needed so its use was confined within that limit. The men got petrol from a pump at the town yard, the site of the old fire station. The limit was 79 gallons per month, which had to do all the mowers and the tractor so the ration was carefully conserved. One way of doing that was to reduce drastically the trimming of fairway grass. The fuel allowance was just 40% of the immediate pre-war levels. If it ran out the machines were stored until the new allocation became available.

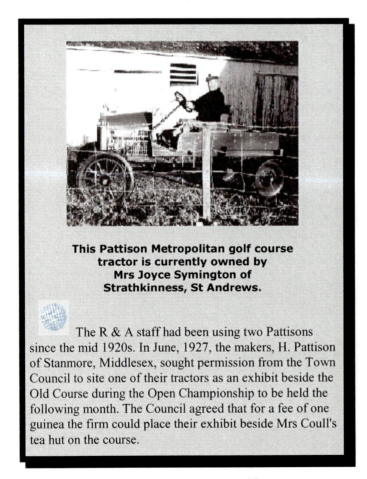

This Pattison Metropolitan golf course tractor is currently owned by Mrs Joyce Symington of Strathkinness, St Andrews.

The R & A staff had been using two Pattisons since the mid 1920s. In June, 1927, the makers, H. Pattison of Stanmore, Middlesex, sought permission from the Town Council to site one of their tractors as an exhibit beside the Old Course during the Open Championship to be held the following month. The Council agreed that for a fee of one guinea the firm could place their exhibit beside Mrs Coull's tea hut on the course.

LINKS WITH THE PAST

During May 1942 the Town Council were required to justify the use of petrol for winter working on the links and argued successfully that their single tractor was kept busy all year round.

There was no resident mechanic employed at the courses in those days and problems with the machines were handled at Central Motors with whom the Town Council had a contract.

With the war in progress the courses were not particularly busy and many of those who golfed were British and American servicemen, some of whom played in uniform. This soldierly association with upright behaviour did not however, prevent a few of them starting at the second tee to get round the courses without paying!

Ladies made up a high proportion of the golfing population at that time.

"In fact it was during the war - 1944 I think - that we first began setting up L. G. U. tees on the courses," said Robert. (It wasn't until March, 1948 that the St Rule Club applied for and received formal permission to place permanent indicators to show L. G. U. tees on the Jubilee).

Golf balls were in short supply and many of those found on the links were taken to local golf outlets like the Forgan shop beside the 18th green of the Old Course, and sold for sixpence, or a shilling for a very good one. The shopkeepers would re-cover the damaged balls, which reappeared for sale bearing names like Goblin or Spitfire.

"You could hardly get the professional-type ball like a Dunlop 65 or a Slazenger," said Robert. "At half a crown apiece few could afford them anyway."

One late afternoon in 1943 R & A worker Tam "Celtic" Melville was cleaning the two 20-inch mowers which were always kept in the hut between the 6th and 7th fairways of the New Course. He was using petrol, the standard procedure, although in his case a certain element of risk applied. "Celtic", so called for his fanatical adherence to Celtic Football Club, was a chain smoker with a difference. He never inhaled. The cigarette just burned between his lips until it began to hurt. A sudden pall of smoke brought other links workers rushing to the scene. "Celtic" had dropped his cigarette and the resultant explosion and fire destroyed both mowers plus the shed. Some flammable parts of "Celtic" had also ignited and he had to make do without eyebrows and part of his hair for some time to come.

The relationship between the links workers and the Army and the Territorials who exercised at the far end of the West Sands was an uneasy one.

"Out at the 9th hole of the Jubilee, which ran right alongside the Eden estuary, were the target butts," said Robert. "There were a number of firing ranges there and when the red flag was raised at the butts you knew to clear off.

LINKS WITH THE PAST

The firing would begin into the target areas, which were constructions of sand and reinforced concrete. These were not removed until after the war."

The exercises being carried out on the beach and on certain parts of the golf courses included the throwing of hand grenades and the holes caused by these mini-bombs had to be filled in regularly. The grenades were stored in lockfast huts to the right of the 1st and 2nd fairways of the Jubilee, along with mortar shells and box after box of .303 ammunition used by both the Army's Short Lee Enfield bolt-action rifles and the Bren guns, the standard British Army light machine gun of the period.

It was the Bren gun carriers racing around on the beach that brought about the worst problems. (The Bren carrier was an open, tracked vehicle used for transporting the guns. The weapon itself was named after the town where it was first produced, Brno, formerly the capital city of Moravia in what is now the Czech Republic).

All of this military activity was going on while the Jubilee Course was being redesigned, a slow, tortuous process which had begun in 1939 and which struggled on till its completion in 1946.

"The Bren carriers would charge up from the beach," said Robert, "and straight across the bunkers which had just been put in for the Jubilee. They were supposed to stay on the beach but the links were nice and hilly and they were tempted to encroach. We had the new greens fenced off but they drove over them anyway. What a mess they made when they executed a turn on the turf!

"Our Supervisor would start to have a go at the Polish drivers but they'd just stare blankly and say: 'We no understand.' They understood all right. You'd seen the same fellows in the pub that night speaking perfect English!"

The Town Council had reacted to one such incident by lodging a claim for damages with the War Department in November 1941.

The manoeuvres on the West Sands had an effect which can still be seen today. Robert reckons that part of the shore has never fully recovered.

> During the First World War part of the links were also used for military training, mostly by the 2/7th and 3/7th Black Watch. The soldiers were granted the privilege of free golf on the Eden Course after 6.00pm. a "perk" acknowledged in a letter of thanks from Major S. Robertson of the 7th Battalion, presented to the Town Council meeting of July 4th, 1916.

"Those high dunes at the far end were torn to pieces by the tracked vehicles," he said. "At one time you could walk through the dunes and be lost to sight."

One hazard for the golfers in wartime was of a pastoral kind - a flock of sheep. They had the run of the links and wandered over all four courses. They were looked after by a shepherd from Balmullo, Dave Harley, who drove them onto the links from the town end. The arrangement had been initiated by the Department of Agriculture (Scotland) in March 1940, in a letter to the Town Council. The Department explained that "nearly every golf course has special value as a grazing subject" and as a matter of wartime necessity the measure was set in place.

Dave Harley had sheep on other courses, including Leven and Lundin Links but they seemed to do best on the 450 acres at St Andrews.

"The animals thrived," said Robert. "And you'd often find them down at the water's edge. They obviously loved the rough rye grass there.

"There were hundreds on the links. They did a lot of damage though, especially round the bunkers. Sometimes one would get stuck in there and it was not unusual to see a sheep and a golfer in the same bunker, employing different methods of getting out!

"Occasionally the sheep fell over and we got them on their feet again and the golfers helped with that too. Getting their droppings off the greens was a regular job for us and we used a wee shovel to remove it. Surprisingly, they didn't harm the greens much. The flock did create tracks however. They'd keep together coming off the courses and you could always see where they'd been."

(STRANGELY THE SCOTS WORD "CADDY" COULD ALSO BE APPLIED TO SHEEP. THIS TYPE NEVER VENTURED ONTO THE COURSES. A "CADDY" WAS A LAMB WHICH HAD BEEN SELECTED OR KEPT AS A FAMILY PET).

The use of the links for pasturage was not new. It had been going on for hundreds of years and it was common for instance during the final decade of the 19th century to see sheep grazing on the 1st and 18th fairways of the Old Course. Grazing was discontinued if complaints from golfers reached a high enough pitch. One such decision was taken by the Town Council in January 1920, much to the disgust of the farmer who had paid for grazing rights. He was not overly concerned when sheep from his farm at Balgove, adjacent to the links, continued to wander onto the courses.

LINKS WITH THE PAST

The May, 1945 meeting of the Town Council agreed to ask the grazing tenant, R. A. Spence of Newburgh, to withdraw his sheep for a week while the Daily Mail Professional 1,500 guineas tournament was in progress on the 19th, 20th and 21st of September. Mr Spence, who had paid a grazing rent of £165 for the year, agreed and was offered an extra week's grazing. His flock comprised about 350 wethers (neutered male sheep) and cross gimmers (one-year-olds). Ewes "and their followers" - an odd euphemism for lambs - were considered troublesome and were not permitted on the courses. In December the Council voted to end grazing and this ancient custom was never revived.

During the period of hostilities there was also a degree of harvesting on golfing ground as part of the national "Dig For Victory" programme.

After another farmer had been offered and had turned down the opportunity to make use of the links turf nursery, Radley & Brown, who managed a farm at Argyle Street where the telephone exchange and a car park are now situated, applied for and were granted the use of the area to plant crops like carrots, cauliflower, potatoes, grain, etc. The ground - approximately four acres of it - was in the shape of a triangle roughly between the 8th and 10th greens of the original Eden Course. (The Eden had been opened in 1914 as the fourth course at St Andrews). The soil was prepared for cultivation by horse and plough in April 1943. Radley & Brown were allowed to work the land free of charge.

After the war donkeys were also corralled in a corner of the turf nursery in summertime. They spent many a fine day transporting the children of holidaymakers along the West Sands and were a regular feature of the Lammas Fair as well.

The domesticated animals were exceptions on the links, which were home to a considerable diversity of wildlife.

One day as the squad was taking their morning break in the shelter beside the second green of the Jubilee a family of stoats appeared.

"There was a male, a female and three young ones," said Robert.

"They didn't bother about us at all. They investigated the hole then took turns in running up the flagstick. At the top they each had a go at the flag and in no time it was reduced to ribbons. You learned to give stoats a wide berth, especially if there were young ones. They could be really vicious." (The stoat is widely held to be the strongest creature in the world, pound for pound).

The golfers' theories on how the flag got in that condition must surely have made some priceless listening.

One of Robert's colleagues, seasonal worker Jim Corstorphine, kept the team amused by threatening to cut someone's throat as he sharpened the "shuck" (sickle) which was used mainly to trim the grass round the rim of bunkers. One day, to illustrate the suitability of his shuck for this purpose, he drew a finger knowingly along its edge. It was sharper than he realised and suddenly there was blood everywhere. To a spontaneous outpouring of unsympathetic mirth the would-be assassin fainted. He was ribbed mercilessly about it for years.

Following the loan of their remaining tractor and four of their employees to the Royal & Ancient Club for two weeks for the sanding of the Old Course in early 1944, the Town Council at their July gathering decided to take stock of their mechanical plant for servicing the courses.

This stood at: Two Pattison tractors (one requisitioned for military purposes), bought in May, 1933 and August 1937; two sets of triple mowers, one bought in July, 1924, the other in 1937; three motor mowers bought in May, 1931 and March, 1934.

The report into the state of the plant made depressing reading.

The 1933 Pattison still in use on the links was "completely finished" as were the triple mowers of 1924; the motor mowers were well past their best and but for the war would already have been replaced. It was agreed that an order be placed immediately, for delivery as soon as the war ended, for a new Pattison, a set of triple mowers and a Ransome Patent Overgreen mower to replace the existing motor mowers.

The railway line stayed in operation right throughout the war, run by the London and North-Eastern Railway Company. Since Robert and his mates did not own a watch between them they got the time from the schedule of trains going to Dundee via the junction at Leuchars.

Robert has vivid memories of one railway drama.

"I was cutting the 11th green on the Eden one day when an aircraft came in very low, swooping over the fairway. It looked like the pilot was aiming to pass under the telephone lines, which straddled the railway track. It turned out to be a student pilot flying one of the small training planes kept at RAF Leuchars and he was obviously showing off. He misjudged his approach and clipped the wires with the tailfin, knocking them onto the track just as the 11 o' clock service was on its way into St Andrews.

"There was no means of warning the driver and the engine churned into the wires, which began to tangle themselves round the wheels. It quickly slowed the engine but in the meantime the poles carrying the wires alongside the line started to tear out and topple onto the rails."

Robert later discovered that the pilot had performed this trick before but nobody ever saw him do it again!

LINKS WITH THE PAST

The Old Course was the scene of another wartime aircraft incident, this time during the 1914-18 conflict. The story surfaced in a letter to the St Andrews Citizen of March 11th, 1950. From Lt. Cdr. (A) C. Draper, D.S.C. R.N.V.R. (Retired), of 2 Conway Street, London W.1., it read: "In April 1915, while stationed at the R.N. Seaplane Base at Dundee my commanding officer gave me orders to land an aeroplane on the fairway to the home green of the Old Course at St Andrews. The incident happened about 11 a.m. The C.O. had sent a number of sailors by road to St Andrews to clear the course. I never knew the reason for the flight because there was a fine stretch of sand adjacent, from which we subsequently made several flights. A few weeks ago I wrote to the Secretary of the R & A to ask if there might be some still around who remembered the occasion and who could add something to it. A story went around many naval air stations that the old greenkeeper died that week but I never had any confirmation of this."

(The story was almost true. An employee of the R & A, Old Course starter Andrew Greig, died on April 29th, aged 57. He had collapsed while mowing his lawn. Greig had been 16 years in the job and was known worldwide as "Greig the Starter" - see front cover picture).

NOTE: There was another landing area close to the 18th fairway of the Old Course. A 1936 Merchants Association map of the golf courses showed a stretch of grass south of the railway line designated an "aeroplane landing ground." This was known locally as the Balgove Airstrip and occupied part of the terrain utilised today for the Balgove and Strathtyrum courses. During the Second World War it was occasionally used as an emergency strip for aircraft limping home to RAF Leuchars.

Mines would drift ashore every now and then at the West Sands or the Eden estuary and had to be blown up by the bomb disposal squad, usually early in the morning when no one was about. On occasion crates of butter or lard or some other goods washed up on the beaches, sombre reminders that just beyond the horizon a desperate struggle was raging upon a sea separating the combatants by a few narrow miles.

Robert did his fair share of cleaning out the Swilcan Burn.

"It was done by hand then - probably still is," he said. "The bottom was sand and it had to be kept clear of silt. If a ball went in, the golfer would have no trouble seeing it and retrieving it."

Also done by hand by an elderly gent, John Cruickshank, was the Himalayas putting green.

"He just had an old push mower," said Robert. "You'd never get anyone to do that nowadays."

Robert came across Cruickshank one day, flat out beside the war-time barrier across the road to the West Sands, which often had a sentry on guard.

"He always cycled with his head down," said Robert "and on this occasion he had pedalled smack into the barrier and knocked himself out."

Motor cycle races took place over the sands once the barbed wire and trenches had been removed during 1944 and these events attracted large crowds. Races took place at low tide and the route was straight out and straight back, roughly the track for the Motor Cycle Speed Championships of July 1939. The races continued to be run for many years after the war.

Among anti-invasion devices on the Old Course itself was a strong point beside the 15th fairway. This was a concrete block measuring 12 feet by 12 feet, which also served as a lookout station. It was demolished in 1945. There had been concrete tank traps strung out the full length of the West Sands and at the end of the war these were blown up by Polish demolition experts. The shattered concrete provided base material for an extension of the West Sands road.

Having worked on the courses all day Robert often played them in the evening with his friends and he became a fine player. While most of their "woods" had metal shafts, almost all their "irons" were of hickory! The clubs were second-hand. At about £2 each, no one could afford to buy a new driver, spoon or brassie.

Robert continued to work on the links until called to do National Service in 1948, then of 18 months' duration but soon to be raised to two years.

> A review of maintenance staff on the links at St Andrews during 1948 revealed 13 people working on the Old and New courses, including starters but not including the Caddiemaster; 13 on the Eden and the Jubilee, including starters, plus four seasonal employees.

Although he did come back to his job Robert left to take up employment with a builder in 1954, the year after his brother Tom came to work on the courses.

And when the 20-year-old Tom did get his start it was with a considerable feeling of relief.

He had recently been paid off from his work as a bricklayer and with employment hard to find in the early 1950s, had taken a "fill-in" job at Jimmy Mair's yard, sawing wood while he awaited the vacancy he was told would eventually appear at the links. Working with him at the wood yard was David Anderson, a school friend who would link up with him yet again on the courses in later years (See The Rabbit Trapper).

LINKS WITH THE PAST

When the position duly came up Tom took the chance to join his brother and his uncle on the workforce looking after the courses. He started on the day before the Coronation of Queen Elizabeth in 1953, so he got the next day off!

As a youngster Tom had shown no interest in golf whatsoever and although he would play a little in later life it was never a consuming passion. As a means of providing him with a livelihood however it would last for 45 years and Tom is the longest-serving member of the links staff still in the land of the living.

In his new job he quickly displayed a knack for operating the Overgreens. These green cutting machines were self-propelled but guided by hand and could cut three times the amount of grass managed by the old motor mowers. They had two rubber wheels and long handles for the operator and Tom spent most of his time trimming the grass on the greens of all the courses.

"The Overgreen took about a yard of a cut," said Tom. "The usual setting was three sixteenths of an inch which was considered a close cut at that time. With the machinery available today they are talking about one 32nd of an inch."

During very dry summers Tom and his colleagues would also spend much of their time watering the greens.

"Each green had its own hydrant and we used 'flick' hoses. In the morning you went out to the green allocated to you and you'd stand there for four hours before collecting the hoses and moving to the next green. Play went on all the time and to minimise disruption you'd usually cut a new hole in the front of the green and concentrate on watering the rear and middle portion. (When a new hole was cut the plug from that hole was simply inserted into the old one). To get the front part of the green watered there were two men on night shift."

During November 1928, while a new drainage system for the links was being installed, a cloudburst on the 23rd caused the Swilcan Burn to overflow its banks. For the duration of that single day, the old stone bridge over the burn was the only object above water on all the area covering the 1st and 18th fairways.

Tom has fond memories of Group Captain Douglas Bader. The former Battle of Britain ace with the tin legs was a regular visitor to St Andrews. And not a man, Tom discovered, to accept help from anyone.

"I noticed him in a bunker one day and I was very surprised to see his caddie just walk away from him. It looked as though he was going to have some trouble getting back onto the fairway so I went across and offered to help pull him out."

"No!" snapped Bader, who proceeded with great difficulty to manage it himself.

"The caddie told me he'd left him there because that was the way he wanted it. He HAD to do it for himself."

Tom also worked part-time at the R & A clubhouse as a handyman and one day he was in the Big Room, where a tie is required.

"I was there to get the big board showing the seating plan to take up to the University Hall for a dinner there when I felt a tap on my shoulder. It was Mr Bader, who pointed out that I didn't have a tie. I apologised and said I was on the point of leaving but he insisted on giving me his squadron tie which I wore until I returned it to him that evening."

The great Australian Peter Thomson - The Melbourne Tiger - sticks in Tom's mind for an encounter he had with his caddie, local man Guy Gillespie.

"They were out at the short 11th during a practice round for the Open," said Tom. "Guy gave this club to Peter Thomson who looked at it in disbelief. 'What do you want me to do with this?'

"Just hit the ba' up tae that flag," said Guy.

"If I do that it'll end up in the Eden!" said Thomson, evidently concerned about the strong following wind.

"Not at all," said Guy. Thomson struck the ball, which sailed miles over the green.

"What did I tell you!" said the exasperated Australian.

"Ah," said Guy, " but if you'd only played a half shot you'd have been all right!"

Tom saw Eric Brown many times on the links and on one occasion had something of a confrontation with the former Ryder Cup Captain.

"I'd been having trouble starting the Overgreen," he said "when Eric Brown told me to 'switch the bloody thing off!' I said I would oblige if only he'd start it up again before he left the green".

"I don't know anything about that," said Brown.

"Well I don't know much about it either so I won't be stopping it."

Tom and the rest of the squad would sometimes find themselves involved in crowd control at the 17th hole during major events.

The 17th posed particular problems and not just for the players.

Tom said: "They could not put a fixed fence down the right side of that fairway because the road that ran alongside the black sheds was in play. If a ball landed there we had to prevent the spectators from using that road and possibly disturbing the ball. We were given a rope which we laid on the ground and if a large number of people were coming we'd pick it up so that it became a hand-held barrier." (The road actually had a name - the Old Station Road - and it was formerly an access both to the passenger railway station and to the goods yard).

Of the characters he met on the links Tom has many a fond memory.

"One old guy, Jock Gibson, who worked mostly on the Jubilee, would often get there by bicycle. On bad days he would shorten the route home by

LINKS WITH THE PAST

cycling the wrong way along Granny Clark's Wynd which bisects the 1st and 18th fairways. One time he was stopped by a policeman who said: 'Come on Jock, you're bound to know this is a one-way street."

"Ah ken that fine," said Jock. "That's why ah'm only goin' one way!"

Jock would also sell golf balls on the courses and one lady golfer approached him and asked: 'Greenkeeper, do you have any balls for sale?'

"Just two madam, and they're not for sale."

The poor woman's face went scarlet and Jock walked away but then it dawned on him why.

"Jock hurried back in a bit of a state and explained that he did indeed have two balls for sale but that he'd promised them to someone else.

"He thought he'd rescued the situation but the lady apologised and said she'd got hold of the wrong end of the stick.

"She went scarlet all over again!"

Tom himself fell heir to many a golf ball, as did all his friends.

"It was really our beer money or pocket money," he said. "When you were working the Overgreens you'd start at the beginning of a course at eight in the morning and follow the holes out. By lunchtime you might be on the fifth or so and you walked in for something to eat. You gave yourself about 45 minutes to walk in and used some of that time to hunt around in the whins for balls. It was the same going back out but there was a snag. You were required to cut nine greens a day and the longer you spent looking for balls the harder you had to work when you got back to your machine.

"I think the most I found in a single day was 12 - good ones that is. You threw away the rubbish. We would take them home and scrub them with Daz then grade them - a shilling each, sixpence and so on. We never had any trouble selling them. Winter was a good time for finding balls if we were pulling out whin bushes. Sometimes you'd find them about six inches into the ground. I once found an old gutty ball but I didn't know what it was so I took it to a golf shop and they gave me £5 for it - a lot of money in those days."

The men had some airborne rivals for golf balls, the kind who didn't bother scratching around in the rough.

"You'd see crows picking up balls from the fairway. They must have thought they were eggs because they always made a beeline for the railway line then drop them onto the track, trying to break them. We picked up balls regularly from the railway and as often as not, that's how they got there.

"Old Tam Blair was a notorious ball hunter. His favourite haunt was the 5th hole of the Old Course, although he also frequented the 10th of the old Eden. The golfers had to play over raised ground and they couldn't see where their balls landed. He hid in the whins with his dog and as soon as a ball came to rest the dog rushed out, grabbed it and dashed back to its master in the bushes. Tam got away with that for years until the links authorities got so fed up that they introduced a ruling requiring dogs to be kept on a leash.

"They couldn't outfox Tam Blair. He kept his dog on a leash all right - only it was a clothes line 14 metres long. However he did manage to get himself arrested after a pursuit across the links by two staff members who had seen him lifting a ball which was in play. Showing a remarkable turn of speed Blair reached the railway line and hopped over the fence onto the track.

"I'm not on the course," he yelled. "You can't touch me!"

While one man kept an eye on him the other walked back to the office and in a moment of divine inspiration called the railway police. The next train approaching St Andrews disgorged two police officers onto the line and Blair was held and fined for unauthorised use of the track.

Blair made money out of players who had not managed to arrange a game (single golfers were not normally allowed on the courses). He'd offer himself to make up a two-ball - for an appropriate fee - and off they'd go early before the starter came on duty. He also caddied from time to time.

Blair was more an unworthy than a worthy. He was even known to lift a duck from the Kinness Burn and have it for his Christmas dinner. He had several convictions for theft and the court's patience with him ran out when he was jailed for three months at Cupar on Wednesday, December 28th, 1954 for stealing a golf club. Sheriff Hamilton described him as "a sneak thief and a menace."

In the days before a golfer had to meet specific requirements before he could be let loose on the Old Course - like proof of handicap or a letter of introduction from his professional - some very odd people indeed turned up to play.

Tom recalls a Japanese group asking the Old Course starter, Donald McKenzie, to explain the principles of the game. Since they were about to tee off it seemed a good idea they should find out. Donald tried to simplify matters by saying the object was to place the ball between the disc and the tee box then strike it towards the flag, which he pointed out in the distance. The one who got the ball into the hole in the fewest number of shots was the winner.

Something must have been lost in the transfer of information.

When Donald called out: "Play away please!" one of them hit his ball and immediately shot off down the fairway in pursuit. He thought it was a race! The rest followed suit.

Even for those relaxed times this was too much for Donald McKenzie who got on his bike and pedalled down the fairway to extract the uninitiated Orientals from the course, from where he directed them to the Jubilee.

When Tom began his career on the links there was more wild life than there is today. Stoats, weasels and sparrow hawks all helped to keep down the smaller vermin like mice and voles. Rabbits were the real menace however (see The Rabbit Trapper) and one of the squad who had been a bit of a gamekeeper -

LINKS WITH THE PAST

Roy Cameron - spent six months of his working year trying to keep them in check. He used a ferret and, during night-time, snares. This practice was frowned upon however and he was always careful to lift his snares before daylight. Rabbits were often sold to local butchers.

Although he did not realise it at the time, Tom discovered buried treasure in a bunker one day. It was a ladies watch, rather old-fashioned with an inscription on the back, which he couldn't make out. He took it to the police station. Meanwhile a very distressed female golfer was scouring the course for her watch, a family heirloom of great sentimental value.

"She was so relieved to get it back she gave me a tenner," said Tom.

Tom had a lot of time for the lady golfers of St Andrews.

"They would never forget to say 'Thanks' when you got out of their way to allow them complete freedom to play their shots. They tended to be much more understanding than the men."

One of the main projects Tom was involved with during the 1960s was the rebuilding of the 'sleeper' wall of the Swilcan Burn from the wooden bridge crossing the 18th fairway to the wooden bridge across the burn leading to the first green - a distance of about 60 yards.

"The original railway sleepers had been cut into narrow strips and over the years had become mostly rotten. The new full-width rowan wood sleepers came from the paper mill at Guardbridge and were all coated in creosote. We also took posts from the railway yard to shore up the sleepers.

"It was winter and Willie Paul and I would jump into the burn wearing wellington boots and sometimes we had to jump through ice. We worked all day without gloves, which were not issued to staff at that time. That job took about two months to complete and I'm proud to say it has stood the test of time."

The old railway line itself, which had run from Leuchars into St Andrews since 1852, succumbed in 1969 to the axe of the notorious Dr Beeching (efforts are under way to have the service restored) but Tom remembers it as the scene of a drama involving a workmate, Frank Willet.

"We had to cross the line with the Overgreens to get to the greens of the old Eden on the other side, where the driving range is now situated. The trains made a lot of noise but in certain conditions you could not hear them over the noise of the Overgreens. I was pushing my machine over the level crossing one day when it was blowing a gale, with Frank following on when I felt the rails vibrating. I shouted to Frank: 'There's a train coming!' but it was too late. The St Andrews-bound engine struck his Overgreen, throwing it off the track.

"Frank was a very lucky man. You could not push an Overgreen from between the two handles - you had to push from behind. I think that's what saved him. Frank reported his accident to Andrew Nicol, who fell about laughing. He wouldn't believe it till he saw the remains of the Overgreen. And believe it or not, its engine was still running."

The railway itself had a narrow escape thanks to the activities of an old lady who lived with her husband in what was known as The Wee Gate Cottage, which stood on the site occupied today by Pilmour Lodge, close by the first tee of the Balgove Course. (Pilmour Lodge was bought in 1999 by St Andrews Links Trust in what the Trust describe as "a strategic move, important for the future integrity of the Links.")

A train driver pulled into St Andrews station and went straight to see the Stationmaster.

"There's definitely something wrong with part of the line," he said. "When we were coming to the wooden footbridge near the second tee of the Eden I could feel the train swaying about."

The railway staff went out to check his report and discovered one section of track held in place by just two wooden wedges. Further inquiries revealed that the old lady had been knocking out the wedges and using them for firewood! The railway hastily switched over to metal wedges.

A timetable dated May 1878 showed eight trains per day leaving St Andrews. Third class return fare to Edinburgh was seven shillings; second class ten shillings and threepence; first class twelve shillings and threepence. As you passed out of the station at St Andrews to walk into the town you were greeted with the following words above the exit:

An entrance into Gofftoon let no one dare to seek
Unless he bear at very least a driver and a cleek

Once while helping to put in new bunkers around the 18th green of the Jubilee during the early 1970s, Tom started to unearth all manner of domestic rubbish - ashes, tin cans, glass bottles etc. Part of that course had been set upon the former town dump, which continued out along the West Sands. In fact, the initial part of the West Sands road is built upon rubbish.

The ever-present problems of erosion at the Eden estuary provided the links workers with steady employment.

"We often had to repair the wall out at the 5th hole of the Eden. Every two years or so we would have to dig it out and put in new sleepers. (The sleepers were part of a batch of 2,000 bought by the Town Council in January 1939 at a cost of 3/6d each).

"If we happened to be turfing we'd check the wall for holes and stuff any we found with bits of broken turf. It was a constant battle to keep out the tide."

Painting the flagsticks was a "rainy day" job.

And at St Andrews there were never any numbers on the flags.

LINKS WITH THE PAST

"It was just white on the way out, red on the way in. Except of course for the 18th, which was always white. I'm sure it's not true but they used to say this happened at St Andrews because the building directly behind the 18th of the Old Course was of red stone."

An old ruined cottage sat beside the mussel road, a right of way that cut across the back of the 11th tee on the original Eden Course. The path was walked or cycled upon by people who gathered mussels from the Eden estuary to use them as fish bait. (The Town Council had a Mussel Scalps Committee whose members and their predecessors had managed the mussel beds for hundreds of years. These were leased to an individual who could then sell them. That person in March 1944 was Mr James Chisholm who paid an annual rent of £40).

The cottage was lived in by a local character, 'Peg' Hutchison who slept there summer and winter. The doors were barred but the windows were all caved in and 'Peg' gained access to the cottage that way. In severe weather Tom or some of the other workers would check to see if he was all right and sometimes found him sleeping in a corner, covered by snow.

His brother Jock had won the Open Championship at St Andrews in June 1921. Jock emigrated to the United States just before the outbreak of the First World War and by 1921 was an American citizen. It was ironic in the extreme that Jock, a born and bred St Andrean, should be the first man to take the Open Championship trophy aboard a transatlantic liner.

He had played attacking golf throughout the tournament and during the first round, holed his tee shot at the 8th and almost repeated the feat at the next hole. (Conditions had been so dry leading up to the tournament that the course suffered considerable damage and had to be closed immediately afterwards for a whole month - right in the middle of the high season).

'Peg' may have been little more than a tramp but the Hutchison golfing genes had certainly not passed him by and he had a nice little earner going behind the 18th green of the Old Course, where the Links Trust shop is today. He'd wait for a suitable American, Australian, or some other visitor to turn up and he'd ask them: "What would you give me if I could hit a ball from here over that building (the Grand Hotel) and land it on the back lawn of the Scores Hotel?" (next door).

The red cliff of the Grand soared abruptly into the sky in front of them and the answer was usually: 'It's impossible!'

"What do you bet me then, that I could do it? I'll match any sum you care to put up."

This was a brazen bet if ever there was one since 'Peg' never had a penny to his name.

"Ah," said the canny ones. "How do we know the ball you hit is the one we'll find on the lawn?"

"Mark your ball any way you like," said 'Peg' and it was often a ball with a pen-drawn logo or initials that 'Peg' would be handed to line up the shot. He'd strike the ball with an ancient open-faced club over the hotel then take his 'client' round to the back lawn of the Scores and there would be the ball. It was said he never miscued which was just as well for the hotel guests.

(The Grand Hotel was sold to the University of St Andrews on the afternoon of Monday, September 12th, 1949 for an undisclosed sum and was remodelled internally to accommodate 100 students in a total of 78 bedrooms. It was initially called Hamilton House although it has always been known as Hamilton Hall. None of this made any difference to 'Peg' whose projectiles continued to clear the building with unerring accuracy).

Tom explained: "He had been a professional golfer and there were those who believed him to be a better player than his brother. He was a good teacher too. I was cutting the green on the 16th of the Eden and 'Peg' was sitting on one of the benches there. A lady appeared and he seemed to take a keen interest in her play. She had all the best gear, sun visor, etc."

"Well my dear," said Peg. "You look like a golfer and you're dressed like a golfer but you never will be a golfer."

"And what would you know about it?" asked the lady.

'Peg' had his trusty old club with him.

"If you wouldn't mind giving me one of your balls I'll show you what I know about it."

He chipped it to within a foot of the pin.

"Just to show you that was no fluke, give me another ball!"

He put that one even closer.

"Now if you don't mind, I'll walk a way out with you."

"By the time the lady was coming back in I was on the 15th green. She asked me: 'Who was that trampy man?' When I told her she said: 'Well, I've learned more about golf in these last few holes than I learned in 10 hours with Lawrie Auchterlonie!" (Perhaps the best-known local instructor).

While 'Peg' was making a few bob by such means his brother was busy making a name for himself as a professional golfer on the other side of the Atlantic. But Jock never forgot his roots and frequently returned to St Andrews. A typical visit was his 20th during May/June 1954 when he stopped off for three weeks en route to Switzerland where he and his wife were due to visit her relatives. His distinctive cream car was as readily recognised in the town as he was himself.

LINKS WITH THE PAST

"Every time Jock Menzies, the course mechanic, heard he was coming he put an old tin bath full of water on top of his coal-fired stove in his workshop and made sure 'Peg' had a bath because his brother always took him into his hotel to stay with him. It was a lot different to 'Peg's' normal lifestyle when he'd often be reduced to stealing a bottle of milk from a doorstep for his breakfast."

'Peg', after several collapses on the golf courses when he had to be taken to hospital, ended his days in Balnacarron Nursing Home in Hepburn Gardens, one of the town's most exclusive areas.

The Old Course was closed for maintenance and essential works on October 16th, 1956 and did not re-open for play until April 1st, 1957. Certainly in the modern era the course had never been out of circulation for so long. Every green received 'special attention' and top dressing; tees were improved and new tees laid; large areas of fairway were patched and bunkers repaired and re-faced. While this work was going on the 18th green could have suffered a major setback. On the morning of February 20th, 1957 two horses galloped onto the green, having bolted from their student riders on the West Sands. The animals were led away by the wife of R & A member Lt. Col. A. K. McLeod. Overnight frost had turned the green as hard as concrete and it was undamaged by the horses' hooves.

Reflecting on his long years on the links Tom reckoned that the biggest change he witnessed was that from walking to motor transport.

"In the early days you walked everywhere," he said. "You raked the bunkers and walked all the way back in for lunch, carrying your rake, spade and big shovel. It was the same procedure after lunch and again when you finished for the day. Nowadays they have to get a Cushman (motorised maintenance buggy) to take them here and there. If you had heavy stuff like turf to move, a tractor did that (the links staff had graduated to four tractors - a Grey Ferguson, two Fordson Majors and an old Davie Brown as a spare) but any stuff left after cleaning out a bunker for example, you had to bag it and carry it to the nearest whins or grass pile to dump."

Tom retired in 1998, still the contented occupant, along with his sister, of the council house in Lamond Drive first signed for by his parents in 1938.

THE GREENKEEPER

It is the top job of its type in golf. The man in whose authority lies the care of the world's most famous strip of golfing real estate has the right, however modest he may be, to assume he has reached the pinnacle of his craft.

Such a man is Walter Woods, upon whose shoulders for twenty-two and a half years lay the burden of producing courses of which the Home of Golf could be proud and on which players from every golfing country could extract a memory to treasure for the rest of their lives.

Walter arrived in St Andrews in 1974 with impeccable credentials.

The first rung on the ladder which would take him to the very top felt the weight of the Woods foot at Tillicoultry Golf Club, Clackmannanshire - The Wee County - where he learned much about the greenkeeper's art.

A Tillicoultry man himself, Walter arrived at the club at a time when there was no such thing as a proper qualification for the job.

"I had no formal training of any kind," he said. "All you had to do was learn, little bits at a time, from other greenkeepers. What the club was looking for was someone who was keen on golf and someone who was willing to work. Broad shoulders and a stout heart if you like."

The nine-hole course at Braehead Golf Club, Alloa was the next step and it provided Walter with his first opportunity to make a major difference. Before he left to take up an appointment in England, Walter had expanded Braehead to 18 holes.

The English job was a lovely parkland course - Stanton-on-the-Wold - where he remained for four years before moving on to his first championship track, Nottinghamshire Golf Club (Hollinwell) where, as he put it, "I got the bug for championships."

What he also got in the college he attended in Nottingham were the basic management skills needed for such a venue so that when the St Andrews post came up, Walter was ready for it.

"Mind you, the education side of greenkeeping was nothing at that time and when I came to St Andrews I realised more had to be done on that front. So I got involved with Elmwood College, Cupar and together we upgraded the education courses available there for greenkeeping. I was chairman of the college advisory committee for 16 or 17 years and became Educational Director for Scotland at Greenkeeping Association level."

Part of his own continuing education process involved travelling to America where he attended the National Conference of Golf Superintendents, studied their methods and became an honorary member of their Association.

LINKS WITH THE PAST

Walter had become increasingly aware that in Britain the science of greenkeeping, with its various localised bodies, was conducted in an utterly disjointed manner.

"I approached the R & A and suggested an amalgamation of the Scottish, English and Irish groups which on their own were going nowhere fast. The club decided to fund this new body, which proved very difficult to set up but in 1987 the Association was formed with myself as its first chairman. We had fewer than 1,000 greenkeeping members. Now we have almost 7,000 and from our headquarters in York we can provide greenkeeping education to any greenkeeper who wants it."

A conference is held annually between British and American greenkeepers and supervisors and that remains today one of the principal bridges built by Walter to advance the skills of golf course management in a truly international way.

Of the St Andrews operation Walter said: "In 1974 it was quite modest. The high demand for golf just was not there. The management team was basically a Secretary - Bob Buchanan - and myself. It was my job to look after the courses and to manage the starters, rangers, etc.

"I had seven people working on the Old Course and six each on the New, the Jubilee and the Eden. We had just the four courses then. There were three starters plus a relief starter, three rangers, a mechanic, a rabbit catcher plus a Caddiemaster."

The relatively relaxed approach however, was about to change, driven forward by an ever-rising expectation of higher and higher standards among those who played the courses and by the need to meet the demand for more and yet more golf.

Former Links Trust Secretary Bob Buchanan played relatively little golf and almost none at St Andrews. So it was something of a rarity when he took part in a bounce game over the Old Course in the company of a visitor and his wife.

Mr Buchanan was a trifle embarrassed when the lady arrived on the 1st tee dressed in a very daring outfit not normally encountered at St Andrews.

The situation was not helped by the presence of a good crowd of onlookers taking in play on the 1st and 18th holes while coming up the 18th fairway, four ladies from a local club were also taking a great interest in the scene on the opening tee.

When the starter called his match to "Play away please!" Mr Buchanan's frame of mind was not at its most tranquil. He swung at the ball and missed it completely.

It was every golfer's worst nightmare - a fresh air shot on the 1st tee of the Old Course at St Andrews!

On the question of standards the Woods view is unequivocal.

"In a place like St Andrews there was no point in having one course - say the Old - in top condition and three of lesser quality. That would mean all the local golfers playing that one course and it would quickly become ruined. So a consistently high standard throughout the courses was vital. The tradition of links golf was also important; the keeping in shape of those fine grasses like fescues and bent grasses on land where salt in the air from the sea is a constant feature. That meant eliminating fertilisers and limiting watering of the courses.

"Take the Americans. They are used to playing lush courses and they come to St Andrews to experience the challenge of links golf. This was always the psychology behind our approach, coupled with maintenance of the tradition of championship golf over the past 125 years or so."

During Walter's long spell at St Andrews he witnessed many innovations in the equipment he had available to handle the task.

"If you saw something new that was obviously going to be of benefit you went after it. We were always very high on machinery and you wanted the best. One thing I was very pleased to see were the improvements being made in machinery for aerating the soil. When you had thousands and thousands of golfers descending upon you year in year out the soil suffered compaction, especially in those areas where people walked onto the greens and from there to the next tees. We were able to acquire new machines to spike the ground with the minimum of disturbance and even later versions could do the same job to the point where you could hardly see where they'd been.

"So far as green-cutting equipment was concerned we moved from hand mowers which I had used earlier in my career to the kind of mechanical mower you can sit on. The job could then be done in a fraction of the time it once took - so important when you had a major event to prepare for.

"Now even the fairways can get a high-quality cut similar to what we would have had on greens years before. When I came to St Andrews there were motor pedestrian mowers and gang mowers pulled by tractors but the really sophisticated stuff was not available then."

When Tom Morris was appointed Keeper of the Green at St Andrews in 1864 he was given the tools to do the job - one shovel, one spade, one wheelbarrow. The main innovation brought about by Tom and his squad of workers was the digging throughout the links of a number of wells which were tapped to water the course during dry spells. Watering was carried out in the late evening or early morning.

LINKS WITH THE PAST

Course management posed particular problems at St Andrews.

"You could fill a bunker with sand, only to find that a gale would spring up and blow it all out the next day," said Walter.

The bunker sand comes from the beach at the West Sands and permission has to be sought from the local authority to remove it. The material is taken at low tide, close to the water's edge and the links staff are expected to make good any unsightly holes on this beautiful award-winning beach.

"The bunker facings provide a different problem. They have to be built up all the time. A typical bunker facing at St Andrews might last just two or three years. Part of the problem is the perpetual spraying of sand onto that soil so that it eventually dies.

"Looking after links turf is a very skilful occupation. You have to aerate a lot as we've discussed and you have to encourage the growth of grasses which have become accustomed to survive in far from ideal conditions. These are poverty-stricken grasses and that's the reason that the look of the courses is not always as appealing as some people would wish to see.

"Top dressing has to be a fine riddled soil with a specified particle size. If you bring in 100 tons of that you can mix it with 200 tons of sand from the beach and that does the top dressing for the greens.

> Top dressing for the greens in the spring of 1939 was detailed as: 40 parts crystalline mono-ammonium phosphate (Type D); 30 parts dried blood; 30 parts sulphate of iron.

"I can say that having played on all types of surface I prefer the links turf. You can play more 'drilling' shots and it teaches you to hit the ball more cleanly off the ground. I always very much like the bounce and run shot you get to play at St Andrews. Once you have that shot in your bag, you can tackle any course. I have played with some pretty good Americans who will almost always hit a wedge at St Andrews when they should be trying a pitch and run. They just can't play it. Putting on the greens we have here, which have some pretty fast borrows, is also part of the golfer's education."

When the Open Championship coincided with the Dunhill Cup, the peaking of the Old Course for these events twice in one year could be an awesome undertaking.

"You had to learn to 'hold back' the course just as though it were a racehorse," said Walter. "Then as the tournament approaches you release it or bring it to the front, heading for the line. You also had to find out how long you could peak it for. How often could you cut a green in one day without stressing the grass? It was just experience. To do this successfully in one year I discovered that the best approach was to have the course at about 75 per cent for the rest of the year so that you could work on the improvements needed for the big ones."

Curiously enough, not all major championships meant the closing of the course for long spells.

"During 1978 the Old Course was still being played just a few days before the Open. On other occasions, like 1995, we were allowed to close two or three weeks before. That was a Godsend. And it's commonplace now. Standards have risen so much that there's simply no going back to the old ways. It's the same with the main courses in Europe and elsewhere. At Augusta National for instance, the home of the United States Masters, you will find absolute perfection. I've played there and I immediately became aware of how difficult was the task of the Superintendent, who had to maintain the 'Masters' standard all year round for his members.

"I am a very good friend of the Superintendent, Mark Benson, who has been here to play St Andrews. Like most of his compatriots, he knows that links courses should be left as links courses and that the problems here are different. I like to think he admires me for what I had done as much as I admire him!

"Talking of different problems I mentioned to Sir Michael Bonallack, the R & A Secretary, after the last Open that if the weather remained calm at St Andrews the course was going to be destroyed by the big hitters. Having been a first-class golfer, he assessed the situation and agreed to take the point further. He got in touch with golf course architect John Salvesen, a past Captain of the R & A and from there the solution agreed upon by the Links Management Committee was to create new tees which would lengthen the course and bring back into play some of the bunkers like the Principal's Nose which had been effectively neutralised by the modern power game. The 6th was altered, more to speed up play, then the 10th, where the competitors in the Millennium Open will find the bunker in the middle of the fairway a threat again, then the 13th was lengthened, bringing back into play all the bunkers on the left. The 15th was next, the new back tee reintroducing the little bunkers there then the 16th and The Principal's Nose. About 200 yards have been added to the course."

Golf and controversy at St Andrews often come as close as a ball sitting on a tee peg. The act of violence which separates one from the other has never found a precise parallel in the relations between the locals and the management of the Links Trust but there has undoubtedly existed a sense of unease, distrust even, which ebbed and flowed according to the nature of the issue. One of the most contentious surrounded the decisions taken in the 1980s to go for a major upgrade of facilities for both visiting and local golfers.

Walter Woods was heavily involved in this modernisation process.

LINKS WITH THE PAST

The Principal's Nose Bunker

"I knew from my membership of the New Club, my life membership of the St Andrews Club and from my knowledge of how the R & A Club worked, that the first priority for the St Andrews golfer was good machinery and good workmen to provide quality courses. But there were other matters that needed addressing. It was felt the visiting golfers were getting a raw deal. Looking at the complete picture it was seen as a matter of regret that there was no clubhouse to put people in; golfers were having to change their shoes at the starter's box; if it rained there was nowhere they could go for a shower; and we were conscious of the need to create an area for office space.

"On the playing side, bearing in mind the rising demand to play St Andrews and the requirement for quality it was decided that the Jubilee should be raised to championship standard. One of the unfortunate sides of this project was its construction while people were still playing the course - a very difficult situation. Another two courses were planned, Strathtyrum and a redesigned Balgove* plus a good practice ground which is the driving range today and is also used for the tented village to house the displays and facilities required for major championships.

> The December 1969 issue of the women's golf magazine Pin High made direct reference to the lack of a clubhouse at St Andrews: " It was a great pity that the wives of those competing in the World Senior Championships last October were given no consideration. The fact that they had come from all corners of the world and then found no clubhouse in which to meet or wait for their husbands is surely a bad reflection on the hospitality of British golfers."

"This was achieved by taking up the ground which had been the first four holes of the Eden, so that course was altered and nowadays that is a very fine course indeed.

"A new irrigation system was introduced, partly as a result of some of the droughts we had had - one bad one in 1976 and another in 1984 when we lost an awful lot of turf. We put in boreholes and an underground reservoir in 1987 containing 357,000 gallons, which could be replenished from the borehole pumps as soon as it was taken out. Then we looked at maintenance. We had just one building and there was a clear need for something better. We decided to install roadways around the courses to make access by maintenance vehicles quicker and easier and to remove them as far as possible from fairways, tees and greens.

"The Strathtyrum and the improved Balgove courses were introduced in the summer of 1993 and a couple of years later the new clubhouse with showers, restaurant, shop, etc. With the benefit of hindsight there were things that possibly could have been done better but we were the people with the responsibility for carrying out these works and we just had to get on with it.

The Balgove was described as a "half course", being a nine-hole beginners track which first saw the light of day during June, 1972 when it opened with a temporary layout.

"While all this was going on it is probably fair to say that the condition of the courses went down somewhat but overall I thought we did not bad. Frankly, some of those who criticised us would have been better off awarding us medals. It is never easy to achieve objectives during a period of such drastic change. And locals never like change, whether that be in St Andrews or in Timbuktu. But be in no doubt, these changes were necessary.

"So far as the management structure was concerned, when it was just Bob Buchanan and myself, that was fine for that time. But more and more people were coming until it could be described accurately as a boom and to cater for that there took place a natural expansion of management. I feel that everything the Trust did emerged from a solid approach to each area of managing golf at St Andrews. And it has been successful."

Walter's recollections of the great players and personalities that have visited St Andrews began with Arnold Palmer.

"Even when he stood a distance away there was a kind of electricity from him. And there was a humbleness too, which made him so similar to you and I. Such a great golfer but you could talk to him, man to man.

"Then Faldo always fascinated me. His ability and his total approach to the game were so impressive. I well remember that incident when he refused to play his second to the 18th at St Andrews during the Dunhill Cup. It was very foggy and although he had just 80 yards to go he wasn't happy with his view of the flag. He was booed by some in the crowd but the man was absolutely right. I recall passing the practice ground next morning and there was Faldo, hitting shot after shot of that distance. He went back onto the course, struck the shot and put it stone dead. That says it all.

"I watched him win his Open at St Andrews in 1990 and I thought at the time he was one of the best golfers the world has ever seen."

Walter met Severiano Ballesteros when he won his Open in St Andrews in 1984 on a fiery course, which perhaps suited the Spaniard.

During 1983 and 1984 Walter and his staff refaced a lot of the Old Course bunkers in preparation for the 1984 Open. Trouble was the extreme heat of that summer dried out the new turf at the bunker edges to the extent that it appeared an ugly yellow - not at all suitable for a course about to be bathed in the pitiless light of TV screens throughout the world. The new turf could not be watered extensively enough to solve the problem since the water supply then was inadequate for the task. The solution lay in an approach to the University of St Andrews where a special green dye was mixed. This was sprayed onto the offending areas and the television images appeared quite satisfactory.

The sheer dedication of Jack Nicklaus impressed Walter.

"Nicklaus turned up weeks in advance of the 1978 Open here and he asked me to walk round the course with him. He asked questions on every hole, about the best line, what wind changes might be expected during July, what wind changes if any, occurred with the movement of the tides. He was so meticulous. And he used all this to good advantage during the final round of the event when the wind did change and of course he went on to win."

From his own professional point of view, Walter recalls with particular pleasure the 1978 and 1990 Opens.

"In my time we had four Opens here and 1978 was a great year to prepare for. The weather was ideal leading up to the championship, the rain came and went like you were turning on a tap. During play there was a nice breeze, the sun shone - just perfect.

"We had a telling remark from Simon Owen, the New Zealander who perhaps ought to have won that Open. He was ahead with just a hole or two to go but his inexperience told and Nicklaus came through to win. Owen said he had expected the Old to be something of a cow patch but was pleasantly surprised to see the top-rate condition of the course.

"1984 was different altogether. It was burning hot. You had to work every hour of the day just to try to keep the grass alive. The course didn't look all that good but it turned out to be a good test of golf."

The 1990 Open went like clockwork.

"It was superb. I was able to use all the experience I had drawn from previous Opens, the weather was beautiful, rain came at the right time, the grass was perfect to cut, the machinery we had did a magnificent job and the staff were getting better and better. 1995 was not so easy. Conditions were not good, the grass wasn't responding as it should have done but it ended up being a very successful Open."

The compliments which flowed in from those ultimate perfectionists, the competing professionals, included words and notes of thanks from the likes of Nicklaus and Faldo. Sir Michael Bonallack, upon whose shoulders fell much of the preparatory work for every Open, whether at St Andrews or elsewhere, never forgot to write to express his appreciation of the efforts of Walter and his staff.

A skill which had nothing to do with golf courses but which proved to be an essential part of the job was diplomacy.

"Frankly," said Walter, "some people go looking for trouble. You had to be so careful all the time. Starting up a mower for example could result in an unpleasant incident. The staff had to be instructed on when it was advisable to switch off their machines, how to stay out of people's way, not to answer if they were yelled at - the kind of thing which unfortunately is so common now."

The job DID have its lighter moments.

Walter heard that the first time Lee Trevino played the Old Course, he had his caddie, Willie Aitchison with him on the 1st tee. Here, the old chestnut about Britain and America being two nations divided by a common language burst into full, magnificent flower.

"What's down there Willie - any bunkers?"

"Naw, but there's a burn."

Trevino drove off then hit his second straight into the Swilcan Burn in front of the green.

"Why didn't you tell me about that?" asked the exasperated Trevino.

"Ah did! Ah telt ye there wis a burn!"

"Burn? What the hell is that? That's a goddam creek!"

An old caddie from Dundee had a different kind of encounter with the Swilcan.

"He must have been about 70," said Walter. "He was wee and round, a real roly-poly character. It was about the beginning of April and very cold, frosty in fact. There were four Japanese golfers and he was desperate to carry the bag for one of them.

"Now this caddie had been in the habit of washing his drawers and hanging them out to dry on the fencing behind the 18th green of the Old Course. We were always giving him a row for it."

However, the instigator of this unseemly practice in such an august location was about to experience a more comprehensive laundering.

"His little Japanese client had hit his ball just beyond the Swilcan, onto the edge of the green. The wee caddie decides to help his man line up the putt and while walking backwards, falls straight into the burn.

LINKS WITH THE PAST

"We fished him out and offered to take him back to the caddie shack to get him dried out. He wouldn't hear of it. He said: 'Jist gie me a fag an' ah'll kerry oan!' "

An American playing off the 1st tee hit such an errant drive that the ball struck the 'U' in the Rusacks Hotel sign, knocking it down. Agitated by his misdemeanour the golfer asked his caddie to go into the hotel and apologise to Mr R. Sacks!

**Cutting a slice of turf from the 18th fairway of the Old Course. Destination Japan.
One of the golf and country clubs there had decided to study the links turf to try to reproduce its characteristics. Circa. 1964.**

Walter had the unfortunate experience of having to disappoint Burt Lancaster on the 1st tee of the Old.

"I had received a letter from an American who had been in the Federal Bureau of Investigation and when he retired from that he worked as a greenkeeper on golf courses. He was coming to St Andrews and he asked if I could arrange for him to play the Old Course. The only time he could play was on the final day of the September Medals, when the R & A had the course. I asked the then Secretary, Keith Mackenzie, if he could be fitted in somehow."

"He CAN play," said Mr Mackenzie "but give the members at least half an hour out before you start. And make sure he doesn't interfere with play."

"When we got to the starter's box, who should be standing there but Burt Lancaster. He'd been hanging around for ages trying to get onto the course. Well, he asked if he could play with us but I had a specific arrangement with the R & A for myself and one other so I had to turn him down. It was quite embarrassing. I met Burt Lancaster a couple of times after that and he was amused to recall how the old American greenkeeper was allowed to play and he wasn't."

In 1954, following a volley of complaints from local golfers about the condition of the courses - exactly the opposite of the view expressed that summer by both Henry Cotton and Peter Thomson - St Andrews Town Council introduced at its August meeting a recommendation that a new post be created, a greenkeeping expert with the title of Links Supervisor at an annual salary of £600 plus a rent-free house. In typical St Andrews fashion this prompted another outcry and before making any decision the Council decided to invite the Sports Turf Research Institute to make a special inspection of the links. The body's two inspectors found the turf to be in satisfactory condition, with several "improvement indicators" and the recommendation to appoint the new expert failed to carry by a single vote.

Of the many people he worked with during his days as Links Supervisor Walter has a particular memory of Davie Kilgour.

"He was the best turfer I ever saw. He seemed to have the ability to patch a piece of ground so that you could scarcely see the join. Davie was extremely proud of his work and could get quite enraged at any suggestion that something wasn't quite up to scratch.

"He always wore this ancient coat which he kept hanging up in the shed on the links. And there was one occasion when he and I were cutting a new hole on a green. I selected where the hole would go so Davie stuck the hole cutter into the ground while I went to take the metal cup out of the old hole. No sooner had I done that than I spotted a mouse running across the green from Davie's direction. It made a beeline for the old hole and jumped inside. It's my belief that mouse could only have come from one place - a pocket in Davie's coat!"

Walter's formal association with the links ended during December 1996 when he retired although he remains involved in an advisory capacity through his own consultancy firm.

Walter admits to a degree of apprehension about the Jubilee, New and Eden courses taking on more of a parkland character these days while the Old still presents the traditional fiery links challenge.

"There is a certain peril in the comparisons which are bound to be made and the long-term worry has to be that the Old itself could be forced to go the way of the others."

Walter is also consultant for the new golf course being constructed at Kingsbarns, five miles down the road from St Andrews.

"Make no mistake," says Walter, "that will be a superb links course, one of the best in Britain if not in Europe. We are hoping it will be available for the

LINKS WITH THE PAST

Millennium, although the weather has held us up a bit. Every single hole will have a view of the sea."

This busy man is consultant to the Portmarnock Club in Dublin among others, is Captain of the Tillicoultry Golf Club, a trustee of the Greenkeeper's Association, a member of the R & A Advisory Greens Committee and until very recently was deeply involved with the technical side of the European golf tour.

Walter was no mean golfer himself, having been a regular county player for both Clackmannanshire and Nottinghamshire. His view, held by many greenkeepers, is that the better a golfer he is, the better his course will be, earning total respect from the members.

From left; Course Mechanic "Dod" McLaren, Walter Woods, and Tom Ritchie.

Photograph courtesy of Ransomes, Sims and Jefferies Ltd.

THE RANGER

Tact, diplomacy - and a hide like a rhinoceros.

Essential attributes for the man at the sharpest end of all the employees on the links in their dealings with the golfing public, the course ranger.

Jimmy McFadyen, St Andrews born and bred, returned to the town in 1973 after serving for 12 years as a fireman in the Royal Air Force and he began his 13-year stint as a ranger the following year, taking up a seasonal post (April to October). The next summer he applied for the job again to the Head Ranger, Andrew Gordon, having been sent to see him by the Secretary of the newly-created Links Trust, Bob Buchanan.

"Whit are ye doin' here?" inquired Mr Gordon.

"I'm looking for the ranger's job," said Jimmy.

"Nae jobs here!"

"But Mr Buchanan sent me along to see you."

"You can start the noo!"

And that was how Jimmy came to be taken on as a permanent member of staff.

**Jimmy McFadyen
1999**

"At that time the rangers walked everywhere," said Jimmy. "There was an electric buggy which never worked and a push bike but no one ever used that. Within a couple of years we had graduated to a Puch moped - one of these bicycles with a wee engine incorporated - but it kept bursting into flames. Then Mr Buchanan got us a couple of motor cycles, blue Honda 50s. The number rose to three when we got a red Honda automatic. They were maintained by the course mechanic, 'Dod' McLaren."

When Jimmy started, the gap between tee times on all the courses was a very scanty six minutes. (This was extended to eight minutes, then in the case of the Old to ten minutes).

"At six minutes, life could be difficult. You could get some real traffic jams out there."

The permanent rangers all wore brown three-piece suits, purchased by the Links Trust from Hepworth's shop at 113 Market Street. The men were measured for jacket, waistcoat and trousers, of which each got two pairs. Rangers also wore red helmets except for seasonal staff, who wore yellow.

Jimmy's working day sometimes entailed starting at about 6.30 in the morning.

LINKS WITH THE PAST

"In the summer you could get golfers out at first light which was half past three. It was our job to collect green fees from them on the courses and if we missed a few we'd sometimes be able to collect the money from the porter of the hotel where they were staying. We'd begin at the 16th of the Old Course and work backwards, collecting fees and giving out receipts as we went. There could be as many as 20 games on the courses at that time of day."

Green fees were handed in to the office once a month.

But the main reason for the existence of the ranger was to keep the courses moving and Jimmy got to learn from couriers and the leaders of overseas groups how to say the same phrase in a number of languages: "Play faster please!"

How this request was received could depend very much on the nationality of the group.

"The Japanese were no trouble at all," he said. "If you asked them to do something they'd do it. It could be quite different with Americans. They'd sometimes take the view that they'd paid their bucks and they'd take their own sweet time about playing the course. You'd have to reinforce the point that there was a time limit to each hole and remind them to keep to it. Sometimes you would ask such a group to let the next game play through and they'd usually agree to that without too much bother."

Jimmy remembers having to ask a man and his wife on the 14th tee of the Old Course to stand aside so that the following game could play through.

"We don't mind ranger," said the man, who produced a bottle of Glenmorangie from the depths of his bag. The couple drank straight from the bottle and it was five games further on before Jimmy could persuade them to get back to the golf!

During the summer of 1919 Mr A Watters, who had lost an arm in The Great War, was appointed ranger on the Old Course to keep off the 1st and 18th fairways those "hordes of people" who used Granny Clark's Wynd to get to the West Sands. The appointment was seasonal only. It was not considered necessary to have rangers on any other course. So few people played then that the Caddiemaster, Mr Fyfe, doubled as the Old Course starter.

Jimmy reckoned his job was really to assist the golfers and he would avoid having to take a firm line whenever he could.

"One of the ways you could do that was to get ahead of a difficult group and watch where their drives went. If someone ended up in the rough you'd throw their ball onto the fairway.

"Our Head Ranger had another method. If he saw a visitor about to enter the whins to look for his ball he'd say: 'Look out for the snakes!' It was all said very seriously, and taken very seriously too. The player would hastily drop a ball on the fairway and hit it."

Many a male golfer has expressed the view down the years - often forcibly - that female players hold up the course. Not so says Jimmy. In fact, the opposite is true.

"Lady golfers seldom seem to lose a ball. They tend to hit short and straight. Men on the other hand are always going for the big shot and they end up all over the place. Men - mostly visitors - were also much more guilty of holding things up by taking reams of photographs. And from the ranger's point of view, the camcorder is the worst invention in the history of the world!"

The first ranger hired after the Second World War was James Low, taken on in June 1945. Mr Low was no stranger to the job, having been a ranger before the war and until September 1940 at which point he was invited to take up temporary service with the St Andrews Gas Company Ltd. It was understood that his job on the links would be kept open. For Mr Low's second stint as a ranger in 1945 he was expected to stand in as a starter. During his first three weeks he took £36 15s in green fees on the courses and in the starters' boxes. He was advised thenceforth to keep the monies separate. In July 1946 two further rangers were added, to work only during July, August and September.

It was very much an unofficial task but the rangers often found themselves on a booze run.

"You could be asked to get beer, whisky, etc for some group and you'd nip into the Jigger Inn or into town to the off-licence that used to be where the North Point Cafe now is. Some of these golfers found it pretty thirsty work! They were always running out of golf balls too and we'd be asked to get them a re-supply."

The rangers' motor cycles were employed in a number of other odd ways. They'd take caddies on the pillion out as far as the 9th of the Old to people who had been unable to find caddies at the start of their round.

If a match had to be removed from the links for persistent slow play - this happened only once in Jimmy's case - the rangers would transport the group's clubs off the course while the golfers went back to the starter to seek a refund.

LINKS WITH THE PAST

There were also times when the rangers had to give people a ride back to town because they were too exhausted to carry on.

"This happened more often than you would think," said Jimmy. "Out at the far end of the courses some older players would find they just could not carry on. I'd either take them in my own car or sometimes on the back of the bike - complete with clubs!"

The motor bikes could be quite difficult to handle in wet weather and in wind and all the rangers came off frequently. Bunkers too, were not just hazards for the players.

"If you were riding along a course 'the wrong way' you could not always see where the bunkers were. We all went into them from time to time, especially the seasonal rangers who didn't know the courses well."

The worst bottleneck on the Old Course was the 7th tee.

"I've seen six games there," said Jimmy, "with their caddies. And if they happened to be R & A members there could be a few dogs as well. As far as I'm concerned the best way to open any busy golf course is with a Par 3. That way you should always get a good start to play.

"One effect on the pace of play has come from TV, with everyone seeing how long it takes the pros to get round a course. The rangers always dread the period following the Open Championship. The courses can come to a near-standstill. You get all this nonsense about using putters as plumb lines, examining a putt from every angle, marking a ball six inches from the hole, etc. It just gets to be a habit and as far as I can see it does no one the slightest bit of good. Then they'd get to the next tee and out would come the scorecards. It never seemed to occur that this could be done between shots. It all made our job much harder and was so frustrating for every other game behind."

The "scattering of ashes" on the Old Course was something which occurred from time to time and Jimmy once undertook this task, scattering the ashes from his motor bike along the fairway of the Bobby Jones hole, the 10th. In this case the deceased was an American golfer who had been planning for years to come to St Andrews but had never quite made it.

Jimmy's job was extended to the point where he was also doing work as a starter.

One day on the Old Course a name appeared on the ballot form - D. R. Bloom. This gentleman appeared for his game wearing a trenchcoat and on his arm, an extremely attractive young woman. It was obvious from the outset that neither had ever played golf.

"They started off on the first," said Jimmy "and played to the 17th green. The woman had taken about 35 shots to get there. We had not long been issued with radios and I called the ranger, Willie Deas, to ask him to take a look.

"Meantime they had played from the 17th and somehow got to the second green of the Old. From there they crossed to the first tee of the New

Course and began to play that. As the day wore on they got lost again and ended up on the Jubilee. It was eight hours before they got back in. Nobody did anything - we were all just so relieved to see them vanish from the Old Course."

Jimmy was present at a million-to-one occurrence on the Old Course.

"One golfer was playing his second to the 7th green while another was driving from the tee of the short 11th. The balls collided in mid-air and dropped down a few feet apart."

Among the personalities Jimmy became acquainted with was Burt Lancaster.

"He was a great chap, and a good golfer too. We had many a chat on the Old Course. I also remember Hubert Green, the American pro. He always spoke and I got to know him quite well."

> At the Town Council meeting of Monday, April 17th, 1950, Police Judge D. Fraser was "astounded" to learn that during 1949 there had been but one ranger to cover all the courses. The man had put in much unpaid overtime to try and carry out what was really an impossible task. It was "entirely in the interests of the town that there should be two rangers on the links" and another was duly hired.

The rangers had various vantage points on the links from where they could see for miles, especially after they were issued with binoculars. These were so effective that the rangers could easily make out the different colours of bag tags from a great distance.

The 6th on the Old was a favourite spot. There was a seat called McNamara's Bench where they'd park for a while and across on the Jubilee opposite the 9th green of the New was another point from where they could keep an eye on things.

During wintertime Jimmy and his fellow rangers helped with maintenance work, painting tee boxes etc.

"We made pre-cast concrete fence posts and the fence behind the 18th green for instance was all done by rangers."

They also rebuilt the wooden bridges across the Swilcan Burn, using a South African hardwood and made all the direction signs on the courses. A frequent task was the retrieving of golf trolleys from hotels and repairing them when required.

LINKS WITH THE PAST

Batteries for the till at the New Course were recharged by the rangers.

"The New Course starter's box had no electricity then," said Jimmy. "The till was operated from battery packs which had to be charged up at the Eden Course and taken to the New. What a weight they were!"

Apart from balls which were found all over the links, Jimmy picked up golf clubs by the score.

"I might hand in up to 200 clubs in a year," he said.

"I even found a full set one day. It was late and I was on till 8 p.m. The rangers had to do that to pick up green fees from golfers going out after the starter had finished for the day. We're talking about tenpence to play the Eden, fivepence for the Jubilee at that time of day - something of that order. I noticed this bag of clubs had been left propped up at the New Course starter's box. When I came back later they were still there. I handed them in at the Police Station and since no one claimed them within six months I got the whole set. I played with these clubs for years - Swilken Tournament they were."

On another occasion Jimmy was talking to a caddie who showed him the clubs he was carrying. They were hand-made, a one-off set. Jimmy had never seen anything like them.

"I was on the bike which was still moving along slowly when the caddie dropped one of the clubs right among the spokes. It just got mangled. There was no way that club could be replaced. I don't think the caddie got a tip that day!"

Of the many balls Jimmy found, two stand out in his memory.

"One was coated with 22-carat gold. I came across it on the 4th hole of the Old Course. Brand-new it was. The other was an electronic effort called the Never Lost Ball. I cut it open and discovered a tiny transmitter in the middle. I think the owner must have had some sort of device designed to receive this signal but in this case it hadn't worked!"

One year, around the 13th tee of the New Course, a colony of guinea pigs put in an appearance.

"Someone must have let loose a couple and they bred worse than rabbits. It didn't last long though. That first winter probably killed them off, or maybe the weasels got them."

It was on that same hole that Jimmy picked up a lot of clubs.

"During the winter I'd go in among the clumps of tall stems around that tee and there I'd find a number of clubs. It seemed that some people were in the habit of throwing away their club after a bad shot and hadn't been able to retrieve it from the vegetation."

Jimmy could never understand golfers who left their putters on a green and never came back for them.

"You'd go to the game ahead to inquire about it and nobody admitted to losing one! How can you do without a putter? It's a club you always need."

In common with some of his colleagues from earlier times Jimmy found the St Andrews crow to be a pretty smart cookie.

"You'd see them following the turfers - the fellows who repaired fairway damage. The crows would lift a patch, look underneath to see if anything edible had surfaced, then drop it again."

There were always a number of people living rough on the golf courses, one of whom was a real mystery man. He lived in a sleeping bag for years, out near the 6th tee of the Old. Jimmy never found out who he was but he came across the bag often enough, always minus its occupant.

"Then there was the four-sided hut near the New Course starter's box which was used by some rough sleepers. As it was open to the wind from every quarter we called it The Four Winds Hotel. Although it was made of wood, this lot would start fires inside it and it became all blackened along the inside walls.

"One of these characters was Fearless Fred, who had caddied a lot at one time. In the end he was banned from every course. He over-charged the golfers and was forever drunk.

"One Saturday afternoon I was standing at the usual high point at the 6th on the Old when I spied him coming onto the New with four lady golfers. He was carrying four pencil bags, two over each shoulder. It was one of those occasions when you closed your eyes and made like you'd seen nothing."

Jimmy McFadyen (centre standing) in conversation with Jack Nicklaus.

LINKS WITH THE PAST

There were also two brothers who caddied on the links and there was always a joke about which of the pair would die the richest for they never seemed to spend any money.

One was called The Camel because he could carry on all day with just a wee bottle of water and a slice of bread per round. Once he'd finished his round he'd take the money he got straight to the bank then go back to work with another bottle of water and another slice of bread. He was never seen eating anything else on the courses. The Camel carried on caddying until well into his 70s. The brothers are now dead, leaving the vexed financial question still unresolved!

Jimmy left the links when the status of the rangers was altered from permanent to seasonal in 1987. There HAD been three permanent posts and two seasonal. No one had a particular course. They worked them all and got to know them all.

But it is difficult to imagine anyone knowing the courses better than Jimmy. In addition to playing them regularly he worked as a ranger, a starter, a maintenance man and during the summer months he even caddied a bit. In golfing terms, rather a full life!

The number of rangers employed on the courses at St Andrews varied with the seasons and according to the view taken by the management of the day. The situation during the summer of 1939 was not unusual. In May there were three rangers, one each for the Old, Eden and New courses. Two of these had just been taken on for the season. Seven weeks later they were paid off.

THE BLACK SHEDS

The Black Sheds, or Railway Sheds, were one of the most famous features of perhaps the best-known hole in golf - the 17th of the Old Course.

There were three of them, plus a brick-built office for the Links Supervisor.

From the 17th tee they provided the line for the adventurous drive aiming to cut the dog-leg of the fairway and still alight in play. The area of the sheds was separated from the course by a low wall. Beyond it, a ball was out of bounds.

One old shed had contained at one time all the material for the Open Championship and other big events - scoreboards etc - and this was moved by truck all over the country depending on where the event was being held. All of it eventually moved to a store in the neighbouring village of Guardbridge.

In another, two railway lorries were stored. These three-wheeled Scammels delivered parcels to local destinations from the adjacent goods yard.

A third shed was used as a workshop by the course mechanic.

It seems likely the sheds were built to complement the coming of the railway in the 1800s and were prominent on an Ordnance Survey map of 1893.

The sheds fell victim to the scalpel of progress when demolition began in late October 1967 to make way for the £600,000 British Transport hotel about to be constructed on the site. The Alcan Golfer of the Year tournament was the last in which the old sheds were a feature. The hotel's original plan for the area occupied by the sheds was to place a gazebo-style tea-room there. However, they had second thoughts and applied instead for temporary permission to raise vertical screening to mimic the silhouette of the sheds. This business was handled for the hotel by its General Manager Mr F. G. Hole, in whose name appeared to reside the broadest of hints about the matchless quality of the 17th. Eventually buildings WERE erected on the same lines as the sheds and were put to a variety of uses, including a golf school, with nets, bunkers etc.

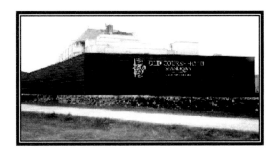

The "New" Black Sheds.

LINKS WITH THE PAST

THE RABBIT TRAPPER

Whether of the four or two-legged variety, rabbits on a golf links can wreak havoc.

While one by means of the equipment he carries carves out his own random designs on the turf, the other by natural instinct can be even more destructive.

Burrows and golf courses do not make amiable companions and any complex which does not include in its staff someone to out-fox the rabbit is failing in its duty to the playing and paying customer.

David Anderson spent 32 years working on the links at St Andrews, the last 12 of those as the rabbit trapper.

"It was my job to cover all the courses and to get rid of as many rabbits as I could. In the days before I took over snares were sometimes used but they could catch dogs as well as rabbits and latterly the approved method involved Cymag, a powder which emitted a gas when exposed to air.

"You'd put a single tablespoonful down the rabbit hole with a long-shafted spoon, then seal the burrow. This had to be done by finding the rabbits' bolt-holes and placing divots over them. Rabbits always had bolt-holes. These were escape routes, for use if the burrow was invaded by a weasel or a ferret. The mouth of each bolt hole was very narrow and a rabbit could easily force its way through. These escape routes were often difficult to find.

"When you used the powder you put it about two feet in. This had no effect until the rabbits began to come out in the evening. Then they'd hit this wall of gas and that was that. You could get up to 30 at a time. Rabbits killed that way were no good for anything and were just left in the burrow."

Dave had to exert care with the Cymag, which could be dangerous to humans.

"You made sure you never used it near buildings or sheds in case some of the gas might seep through the floor."

The rabbit trapper took his work seriously and even invested £300 of his own money in a .22 BSA air rifle which he bought from Gows of Union Street, Dundee.

"You weren't allowed to use a shotgun," said Dave "but the air rifle did a good job. I'd drive along slowly in the car about five in the morning to get close to the grazing rabbits. They'd disappear if they saw a man but a car never seemed to trouble them. I'd wind down the window and shoot them. Sometimes I'd end up with as many as 30 dead rabbits in a sack. These you COULD find a use for. Mind you, they weren't always as dead as I thought and the sack would start dancing!

LINKS WITH THE PAST

"At that time on the links there were a number of pensioners employed part-time during the summer doing various jobs and I'd offer them a choice from the sack. They'd say: 'I'll have that one for the pot' or 'that'll do for the cat'."

Dave was not averse to taking a rabbit home and cooking it and he also kept a few of his neighbours supplied, including a policeman who had once been a gamekeeper himself.

Dave not only enjoyed the independence his job brought, he was in no doubt about its worth.

"If there were no rabbit trapper, the links would be over-run in no time."

Worst area for rabbits on the links land were the mounds on the Jubilee Course. There was plenty of scope for them there and they were hard to get at because of the concentration of whins and gorse bushes.

Rabbits would also invade bunkers from time to time, especially to scrape a den in which they could have their young.

"Hell Bunker on the 14th of the Old Course was a favourite spot for them," said Dave.

Moles posed a different problem.

"You could use the gas on them too but I always liked to know I had actually got them and I preferred a proper mole trap. It consisted of a metal tunnel about six inches long with a tongue inside and you'd set it along a known mole run. Moles always dig in a straight line. The weight of the animal on the tongue triggered a wire which killed it."

Dave recalls a five-day battle of wits with a rogue mole.

"This one was causing havoc on the new 5th green of the Jubilee. He wasn't tunnelling deep and you could see the raised grass where he'd been. I couldn't understand where he'd come from since the nearest concentration of moles was about a mile away out at the far end of the Eden Course.

"I tried everything to catch him without success. I was so worried that I spent £2 of my own money on smoke pellets and tried to smoke him out. No luck. However, on the fifth day, a Saturday which was my day off, I was on my way down there early when one of my colleagues shouted across: 'You've got him! I checked the traps this morning.'"

Strychnine poison was at one time employed on the links to kill moles but that practice, though very effective, was discontinued.

"Moles eat their own dead," explained Dave. "It was said you could kill up to seven with a single dose. A worm coated with strychnine would be set as bait. The first mole to eat it died, then that mole was eaten by another which died and so on until the effect of the poison was spent."

Deer could be seen occasionally racing across the links, having crossed the Eden estuary at low tide from their habitat in Tentsmuir Forest but if that was a rare sight, the street-wise crow was an ever-present.

Dave reckons that of all the forms of wildlife that inhabited the area, the crow was the brightest.

"You could walk up to a bunker with a rake in your hand and a crow would be pecking away at something a few yards away. But if you had a gun, even if it was concealed, you could not get within 50 yards of one. How they knew is beyond me."

They could be troublesome on the greens. In trying to winkle out leatherjackets (the larvae of daddy longlegs, or craneflies) just beneath the surface they often caused damage. Dave discovered that if you were able to shoot one using the rabbit strategy of approaching slowly in a vehicle, you could place it beside a green in the knowledge that no other crow would land on that green.

Dave has mixed memories of his encounters with the paying customers.

"They'd often think I was hunting for golf balls. The Americans would call me a 'ball hawk' and I had some amusing exchanges with them but what did annoy me were the nudges and whispers from people who obviously thought I was scraping around for balls for a living."

Inevitably though, Dave did come across a lot of golf balls in the course of his work and found some in the oddest places.

"I think the strangest was the brand-new ball I saw sitting right in the middle of a bird's nest. It had clearly been a wayward drive from the 6th tee of the New. It was odd too, how you could pick up a ball in the whins only to discover it was sitting exactly on top of another, almost buried ball.

"On one occasion when Mr Campbell, the Supervisor, decided to straighten out the roadway round the 5th hole on the Old Course, I had to help pull out some whins by tractor and chain. We came across eight old gutty balls. Some must have been nestled down at the foot of the whins for 100 years and more. We never thought anything of it but nowadays these balls are very valuable if they are in good condition. Occasionally you'd find one half buried. The top had virtually disintegrated but the half under the ground was like new."

When the Irish singing group, The Bachelors, turned up to play Dave had a little exchange with them that fell rather flat.

"As a bit of a joke I said I hoped they'd be better on the golf course than they were on TV but that didn't go down too well!"

Another time four English ladies were playing near where Dave was working with a spade.

"One of them asked me what I did and I told her."

"She said: 'Do you hit the rabbits with the spade?'"

"Oh, aye," I said. "I stand beside a warren and make a noise like a lettuce. When the rabbits come out I hit them with the spade."

As the ladies continued their round they were still animatedly discussing this revolutionary method of pest control.

LINKS WITH THE PAST

Although not a golfer himself, Dave's intimate knowledge of the terrain could prove invaluable to the players.

"I'd often see someone lining up a putt wrong and would set him straight. They'd ask me to go all the way round with them but of course I couldn't."

An 80-year-old St Andrews lady, who was diabetic, gave Dave quite a scare one day when she collapsed on the course.

"She had forgotten to take her insulin. However, I was able to drive her to her home just opposite the Post Office in North Street. She looked terrible and I was really worried about her. Next day I was working as usual, at the far end of the Jubilee about seven in the morning when I saw her there, walking her dog!"

Dave was on hand about noon one day when a lady player fluffed her shot on the first hole of the Old Course into the Swilcan Burn.

The level of the water was quite low and Dave fished out the ball. She tried again with the same result. This occurred several more times, Dave patiently retrieving the ball until finally he reminded her that at that time of the year it was liable to get dark quite early!

He was also present during a discussion between the Supervisor and one of the rangers about slow play.

"There happened to be a fellow playing close beside us who had a huge beard. I couldn't resist it. 'See him?' I told the Supervisor. 'He was clean shaven when he started out!'"

The rabbit plague Myxymatosis had been introduced before Dave became the trapper and although it died down, it reactivated from time to time.

"It was horrible," said Dave. "I never liked to see rabbits in that state."

After the disease took hold the familiar sight in butchers' shops of strings of rabbits hanging up for sale became a thing of the past. By November, 1954 Myxymatosis was being described as "endemic" but 13 months later a letter from the Eastern Agriculture Executive Committee was read to a meeting of St Andrews Town Council. The Council's attention was drawn to the designation of Fife and Kinross as a rabbit clearance area and their co-operation was requested in ridding the district of rabbits. Council staff were "instructed accordingly."

Dave's career on the links began on August 24th, 1962 and many of his fellow workmen were former ploughmen or farm hands. At that time there was just one ranger employed - and in a seasonal capacity at that. This Lone Ranger literally kept an eye on all the courses, since he only had one eye.

There was no issue of clothing for employees - they wore their own clothes - but eventually a uniform was introduced, then boots, then gloves, then wellington boots, then wet weather gear.

LINKS WITH THE PAST

"One chap pointed out that we shouldn't accept the waterproofs because it meant we'd be sent out to work in the rain. He seemed to have forgotten we were expected to work in the rain anyway."

It wasn't long before the men acquired a hearty dislike for the waterproofs.

"They were cheap nylon," said Dave. "After an hour of heavy rain you were soaked to the skin anyway and you sweated so much inside them too."

Dave's father had also worked on the courses, in the 1920s. His mother had been employed there too in the premises at Pilmour Cottage, so the young David Anderson was a true son of the links.

Dave's father had started work at a time when the mowers to cut the fairways were towed by horse. To minimise damage from the horses' hooves, the animals wore specially made leather boots. The horses worked mostly for the Town Council's Cleansing Department and were stabled at a yard in Kinburn Park. The Council earned up to £20 a year by selling the manure to farmers and to gardeners. In September 1920 the local authority opted to purchase two new horses to replace a pair "which had been in the possession of the Council for a number of years. They will be disposed of."

Following an inquiry eight years later from the Royal Scottish Society for the Prevention of Cruelty to Animals, the Council stated that they did not keep horses until they were "totally unfit." They were sold for farm work when fresh animals were bought.

In the early days of his employment with the Town Council, Dave would often have to take a mower, drawn by a tractor, through the town to the East Bents Putting Green near the East Sands to cut the grass and relocate the holes. This served as practice before a grass cutter was let loose on the greens of the golf courses. (An ancient grazing right was sometimes invoked on the East Bents Putting Green and during August, 1917 for example, six cows were regularly grazed there).

Dave was also involved with the same work at the Bruce Embankment Putting Green[1] where on one occasion he accidentally picked up in his cutting machine one of the metal arrows pointing the way to the next hole. The machine had to be taken in to the workshop for repair and Dave's foreman, Roy Cameron, was not a happy man.

"Didn't you see the arrow?" he asked.

"Arrow?" said Dave. "I never even saw the Indians."

LINKS WITH THE PAST

[1]The Bruce Embankment had been known as The Boat Embankment before its change of name in January 1897. The new name was in honour of the man who reclaimed it from the sea, Councillor George Bruce. Bruce, a builder, had seen the possibilities of this stretch of sea-washed beach but had failed to get the Town Council interested. Undaunted, he determined to fund and carry out the work himself. Bruce had four old boats towed from the harbour, moored them stem to stern at the west side of the beach then filled them with concrete and heavy stones. To the east of the boats, as a foundation for this part of his reclaimed area, he created a sloping barricade of stakes driven into the foreshore. Bruce then invited St Andreans to use the area as a rubbish tip and it gradually filled up to the point where it could be consolidated and properly surfaced. After a number of setbacks the project was completed and Bruce lived long enough to see one of his main ambitions for it realised - the siting there of the Lammas Fair. The putting green occupying the site today, which first opened for play on July 2nd, 1914, has often been described as the best in Scotland. Original fee for playing the course was one penny.

Dave enjoyed working with all his colleagues.

"Once I went to the rabbits though, I'd tell them: 'You're lucky to have each other to talk to. Look at the company I have to keep!"

One odd job which had to be carried out periodically was the removal from the local slaughterhouse of offal, hide, etc. This unsavoury cargo was held in a tank to which a tractor was hitched. It was then towed through the town to the golf courses where it was used for compost.

"It would be dumped in a pile then covered with earth or sand and left to rot," said Dave. "The only trouble was that if it wasn't covered well enough the seagulls got at it. You could get a group of golfers suddenly coming across a bull's privates in the middle of a fairway."

Dave recalls one old chap whose sense of direction was so bad that if he was instructed to go to a tee which needed some attention - say the 5th on the Eden - he could never find his way straight there, even though he'd been in the job for years.

"He would follow the tee boxes, one, two three etc, till he finally got to where he was going. He'd walk about twice as far as he needed to.

"Another man got into the habit, if he was out at the far end of the Eden, of crossing the field to the main road and waiting for a bus to take him back to the goods station where the black sheds were. Anything to avoid the walk back."

Dave got to know several caddies and has a particular memory of one.

"He was always very proper spoken and would unfailingly give the impression he was a lot better than you. One day I was working on the 16th tee of the Old Course when he and his golfer - an American - came onto the tee. I stood

LINKS WITH THE PAST

aside and propped my spade against the railway fence, only to be told by this caddie that I should have laid it flat.

"You can't get the staff these days," he told his golfer.

"That was too much for me. I went straight up to the American and said: 'Excuse me sir. If this man was half as good as he thinks he is, you'd be caddying for him.'"

Dave liked to take his break on the seat at the short 5th on the New Course if the weather was fine and he had many a chat with the golfers.

"One American pair asked me what club to take and I told them a local group had just played seven irons, the wind being the way it was.

"Nothing like local knowledge," said one as he prepared to play. His shot failed to reach the green and he came up to me and said: "That finished about 20 yards short!"

"Aye," I told him. "So did the lot in front!"

Of all the excuses trundled out by golfers at St Andrews the most common in Dave's experience is: "I didn't quite catch that one...."

When Dave began in 1962 the caddie situation was such that some of them slept rough, in shelters and the like.

"It's different now but I can remember one fellow who caddied a lot and who slept in the shepherd's cottage that used to be behind the 3rd green of the old Eden Course. The floor was just earth.

This building had been scheduled for demolition but the Royal Air Force at Leuchars said it was such a good mark for their incoming aircraft that they asked it be left intact. The house had been occupied, but not continuously. Its drinking water supply was provided by a well located right under the centre of the 3rd green. In September 1926 it was discovered that the water had become contaminated. The building is now a toilet block behind the 1st green of the re-designed Eden.

"On one occasion in 1967 I found this fellow in the Eden Pavilion dressed from head to toe in the usual smelly gear, coat with upturned collar, scarf, bunnet, the lot. And he was attempting a wet shave. I suggested it might be better if he discarded some clothing but he said: 'Na. Ah'll jist dae the bits they can see!'"

In common with his mates, Dave especially enjoyed working on the Old Course.

"There was a definite status about it and it wasn't uncommon for someone who had done something wrong to be threatened with banishment to one of the other courses."

There were specialised tasks to be undertaken when an Open was due and Dave's work was always seen on TV.

LINKS WITH THE PAST

"I had to paint the hole cups white so they'd show up well on television. It could be the very devil of a job, with the rim of fibre above the cup always catching the brush."

Dave had a successful if unofficial stab at cultivating part of the links.

There was a piece of ground at the outer edge of the Eden Course near the old railway line which was not well drained. Some of the earth was dug out of this area and the gaps filled with pebbles. The spoil was removed by cart and dumped just off the fairway.

"Nobody ever trampled on it and it was nice and soft," said Dave.

"I got the offer of about 40 seed potatoes - Duke of York I think they were - and planted them there. We then had a very dry year and I never believed they'd come to anything although of course, potatoes ARE a sun crop. But in August I dug them up and they were the best I'd ever seen. Not one was smaller than my fist. I harvested enough of these to fill three plastic sacks and took them down to the maintenance sheds. Everybody wanted some and I went home with just a small bucketful for myself. They were absolutely delicious."

Over the span of his years on the links Dave noticed a massive rise in the numbers of people playing golf.

"It wasn't just that the game was becoming more and more popular. When I started, one week's paid holiday per year was standard but people began to get much more leisure time and they spent a lot of that on the golf courses."

Time on the courses extended to about half a lifetime in Dave's case and when he at last called it a day in 1994 it was on November 18th, his 65th birthday.

His speech at the retirement presentation ceremony in Pilmour Cottage, the administration centre on the links, was one of the shortest and best received of its kind.

"I spent 33 years here," said Dave "and nobody ever listened to a word I had to say. So I'm not going to say anything now!"

FOOTNOTE: Getting rid of rabbits on the links was an activity in complete contrast to how this ground had been worked in the past. On several occasions the links at St Andrews had been utilised for rabbit farming, notably during the early part of the 19th century. The meat and hides were sold for profit. This practice very nearly ruined the links for golf.

FORE!

In no other game are those whose livelihood depends upon it more at risk than golf.

Think about it.

Every day on a busy golf course thousands of stony projectiles rocket through the air, propelled in many cases by people who have but the vaguest notion of what they are doing.

The links workers are in a real sense under fire.

Come the end of their careers, a more appropriate retirement gift than a painting or a clock could be an active service medal.

ROBERT RITCHIE calls to mind an occasion when he was driving a Fordson tractor, bought by the Town Council from the R & A in the spring of 1946 for £240.

"I was approaching the 3rd hole of the Eden. The vehicle had no floor - you just stood on the footplate. I noticed this golfer taking a practice swing on the tee - or so I thought.

"A second later a ball struck me full on the forehead. Somehow I managed to stop the tractor, which was heading for a bunker but I was almost knocked out.

"I tried to carry on working but kept having to sit down. Finally my uncle came on the scene and immediately sent me home. Mind you, that meant cycling home. How I got there I will never know. My head hurt for about three weeks."

For a while cages were placed on the tractors to prevent the same thing happening again but these were later removed.

**Robert Ritchie
on a 1953 Ferguson Diesel**

LINKS WITH THE PAST

One colleague of **JIMMY McFADYEN**, Ranger Bill Duncan, was on the 4th tee of the Old Course, talking to an American golfer when someone teed off the 2nd of the New. The shout of "Fore!" came too late and Bill was hit full on the side of the jaw, shattering his false teeth.

While Bill was taken to hospital for a check-up, the remains of the teeth were consigned to the tee box.

Two weeks later Jimmy was on the same tee, talking again to some Americans who had obviously heard what had happened.

"Are you the ranger who got his teeth knocked out?" they asked.

"No," said Jimmy "but let's have a look in that box."

The teeth were still there.

Jimmy was hit several times himself but his most excruciating experience was self-inflicted.

"I golfed on most days, sometimes just a few holes at a time. This time I smacked a ball into a whin bush and it rebounded and hit me on the face. Broke my nose!"

DAVID ANDERSON recalled the gentleman who played St Andrews regularly, two or three times a week.

"He was a very pleasant chap," said Dave. "Always had a cheery word for you."

One day he was playing with friends and after he drove off, he strayed a little too far in front of the tee. As the next player hit his shot he turned to say something and the ball smashed into his mouth, driving right through his teeth.

"He was quite badly injured," said Dave. "His teeth and gums were in a terrible state."

The man was never seen on the links again.

FOOTNOTE: Some of the petrol-driven buggies used by today's staff carry heavy-duty protective screens of transparent plastic and indeed this practice is now standard on the driving range.

THE OPEN CHAMPIONSHIP

Since the Second World War St Andrews has played host to 10 Open Championships. After July 2,000, it will be 11.

And no book about golf in the cradle of the game could hope to be complete without a major reference to this, the definitive Major.

However, rather than have a dart at covering them all and spreading this richly-flavoured jam too thinly, I thought it better to take a single Open and within reason, let the detail flow.

But which to choose? The Lema triumph of 1964 when he won by five shots having turned up in time to turn in the barest of practice sessions? The Sanders/Nicklaus drama of 1970? Faldo's record-breaking win in 1990?

I have a confession to make. On a level that has far more to do with instinct than logic I find myself firmly on the side of those who mourn the passing of gentler days when the game was still a game and far less of a business. This is not to deny the need for improvement and change, for golf itself has altered almost beyond recognition, but rather to recoil from much of what has come with it.

Marketing men in sharp suits; brash, intrusive advertising; so-called advances in club and ball manufacture which have effectively destroyed some of the world's greatest courses; hard-headed and hard-hearted accountants who seem to have the last word on virtually every aspect of our modern lives.

There is just no holding back this tide which eats into the very soul of golf without realising it, or without caring how many of the game's foundation stones are gradually working loose under such myopic pressures.

The rising numbers of players notwithstanding it is a matter of seeming inconsequence that ordinary folk, tradesmen and their like, find themselves increasingly marginalised by the very sport into which they first breathed life as green fees and subscriptions at more and more venues stretch ever further beyond their means. Even the drive for quality, laudable as an end in itself, serves in part at least to mask an underlying trend towards golf complexes of an exclusive hue.

This profit-driven approach bears with it in the stream essentially corrosive sediments and is it fanciful I wonder to detect here a link with what is now widely recognised as an alarming rise in selfish, aggressive behaviour on the golf courses?

The palmier days which some of us continue to recall with a dampness of the eye found themselves well addressed by Mr Bernard Darwin who, in the September 1949 issue of the magazine "Illustrated" could write: "Of all golfing places in the world, St Andrews is the most democratic. It is a delight at the end of the day's play to see the butcher, the baker and the candlestickmaker, their toil

LINKS WITH THE PAST

over, shouldering their bag of clubs and coming out to play over their very own links."

I make no apology for preferring to look back with nostalgia into the relatively distant past rather than over my shoulder at the sumptuously-staged Opens of the late 20th century.

My choice of event - 1946 - is conditioned not simply by a longing for a lost, innocent era in golf. It is that it took place in a different world.

Man was still 23 years shy of going to the Moon and on the first tee you could unwrap the paper from an object of similar shape - if you could find one - to reveal a name like Dunlop 65 or Penfold with its wonderful heart, club, diamond or spade logo subtly suggestive of the need to think and gamble your way round the course.

At Wimbledon the 6' 7" Frenchman Yvon Petra, wearing long white flannels, was about to defeat the Australian Geoff Brown to take the singles title.

Food rationing was in force and people formed long queues in the dawn chill waiting for bakers' shops to open to buy the allowance of four rolls. Further down the queue waited in dread those who feared the shop might sell out before they reached the counter. To deal with the concerns of a genuinely hungry population, the Ministry of Food was about to open premises at 114 Market Street, St Andrews. Food rationing was destined to last until 1954.

Paper was in such short supply that Golf Monthly had to apologise to its readers in the April, 1946 edition for being unable to carry advertisements for the Open. The shortage did have one beneficial effect - during the Championship there would be a noticeable absence of litter!

The state of national prostration brought with it the equality of want and people went out of their way to help one another. A bowl of soup for the old lady next door. Ragamuffin children running errands for the elderly and the housebound. Rare luxuries shared out as far as they would go. Compared to the pathetic drawbridge mentality of our present age the comradely concern of the 1940s positively glows.

During 1946 Captain W.S. Blunt, formerly of the Gordon Highlanders, visited his native St Andrews to discover that he could not buy a golf ball anywhere. In an interview with the St Andrews Citizen on August 31st, Blunt said: "I am amazed that in a city where the people are practically dependent upon golf for their livelihood, it appears to be impossible to purchase a golf ball."

The Captain may not have looked quite hard enough but his comments bore stark witness to the threadbare nature of the times.

In the course of a game on the Old Course in April, one incensed golfer accused his caddie of stealing a ball. The incident was considered so serious that when the formal complaint was lodged with the Town Council they decided to involve the police. Reluctantly, the golfer withdrew his complaint.

The Open's many amateur competitors felt the chill of this scarcity at first hand. The Dunlop Rubber Company were able to make available for all of them just 24 dozen Dunlop 65s, use of which were to include practice sessions. The company suggested no more than two balls each for the first and second qualifying rounds, one to be played over the Old, the other over the New.

There is a further reason for selecting 1946. The Open that year ran a parallel course with a huge issue of the day for St Andreans - the spectre of green fees for the townspeople for the first time in their long history of playing the game. *

Many of the competitors in the 1946 Open were picking up the pieces of careers disrupted and in some cases ruined by six years of war.

Among the first to arrive in St Andrews out of 264 original entrants (not everyone turned up) were the Spanish pair Mariano Provencio Sanz and Marcelino Morcillo Aberran. They spoke not a word of English between them and during their first practice round on the Old Course on Monday, June 24th, they were accompanied by an R & A member, St Andrews Town Councillor W. P. A. Tulloch who translated for them the advice and instructions from their caddies. (There were 28 licensed caddies in St Andrews during 1946). On behalf of these two competitors the R & A, meticulous as ever in organising the tournament, sent a copy of the local rules to the Spanish Embassy in London for translation. However, neither player survived the qualifying rounds.

Henry Cotton too, had arrived that day and played 18 holes in the afternoon. Seen in practice also were 1936 champion Alf Padgham and Max Faulkner. Dai Rees, winner of the recent Spalding tournament, had a cold. Choosing discretion at the expense of valour he put his feet up and stayed indoors.

American legend Samuel Jackson Snead arrived by train on the morning of Friday, June 28th, along with three of his compatriots, Johnny Bulla, Joe Kirkwood and Lawson Little. The transatlantic contingent was a long way short of what had been indicated by the U. S. P. G. A. who gave the impression that Gene Sarazen, Tommy Armour and Lloyd Mangrum would be entering. Ben Hogan's name had also been mentioned.

Despite what had been a tiring, frustrating journey, Snead practised furiously as soon as he arrived. The ball-starved Scottish spectators gaped in awe as he drilled scores of brand-new balls over the Bruce Embankment and onto the distant sands, where a band of caddies scuttled around like crabs on the beach retrieving them. Snead began his first practice round late that morning and immediately struck a controversial note by criticising the course. (There HAD been some concern in the spring over how the course would hold up during the Open. A five-week drought was beginning to cause real problems before it broke with a cloudburst in the middle of May and by the time the Open came round the

LINKS WITH THE PAST

course was in fine shape. Snead however, was probably more concerned about the layout).

Throughout Snead's stay St Andrews would be treated in equal measure to the sweetness of a swing designed in Heaven and the raw observations of this sometimes viperish West Virginian. He would call the Open "just another tournament" and would refer to the winner's purse of £150 as "derisory." In this latter respect he was undoubtedly correct.

While the game today might be awash with venture capital aiming for lush returns in the world of the well-heeled, it suffered then from a desperate lack of cash where it most needed. In Britain at least the Open was held to be the most prestigious golf event in the world and its pedigree ought to have placed that assertion beyond doubt. The monetary rewards however, reduced its standing to that of a bad joke. Even the winner, if he had to travel to this country, could not hope to clear even basic expenses from his cheque. Endorsements of clubs and other spin-offs would see HIM all right but even with a meritorious second place the overseas golfer was always going to be well out of pocket. It was a deplorable situation which lasted for years. The event routinely failed to attract the top Americans and went into a near-terminal decline.

During these times it was kept going by not much more than its aura and tradition, which managed to retain a certain pull however. Bobby Locke was a fan. During April, 1946 the great South African, in an interview with the Johannesburg Sunday Times, was warm in his praise of the Old Course as "a unique test of golf."

Locke went on to say: "Scots consider the Old Course the only one made by God, the rest being man-made."

He recalled his troubles at the 14th during the 1939 Open when during two rounds he took 14 strokes there, several of them in Hell Bunker. His chance of winning, at one time bright, faded away.

When the 1946 Championship got under way, Locke was once again to mount a formidable challenge - and to experience a change of mind.

Meanwhile, preparations for managing spectators were proceeding, and not without comment.

Earlier in the year Colonel M. E. Lindsay, Chairman of the R & A's Augmented Green Committee, pressed for and gained approval for a whole new system of regulating crowds at major events. For the first time ever fencing and ropes would be used to prevent disruption of play. The old method, which was hardly a method at all, had allowed almost unfettered access by unruly crowds to all parts of the course while play was in progress. Competitors were frequently caught up in the melee and delays ensued. There was also the very real possibility of injury to the players.

In support of his position Colonel Lindsay referred to the "absolutely chaotic" closing scenes of the 1927 Open, won by Bobby Jones. The American had been swamped by spectators to the point where he actually disappeared from view. During the final round of the 1939 Open, Henry Cotton had been five under fours standing on the 14th tee. Such was the size and enthusiasm of the crowd that Cotton was forced to wait for 25 minutes as they were shepherded beyond the out-of-bounds wall to the right of the fairway. This nerve-jangling hold-up clearly affected him and his challenge faltered.

Lindsay's bold experiment was put into practice during the Spalding event over the Old Course in early June, delivering an average separation of spectators and players of 20 yards but crowds were not big and as the Open approached the jury was still out on the new system. Lindsay showed he was prepared to be flexible and decided the onlookers did not need to be that far back.

When it was realised that the ropes were being moved much closer to the fairways than they had been for the Spalding, disaster was confidently predicted in several quarters. By the end of the Open however, the arrangement had proved itself a great success. The R & A did not crow and the prophets of doom did not acknowledge their own lack of judgement, melting silently away in the manner of all their kind.

> Although it was scarcely comparable, a type of stewarding with ropes HAD been tried at St Andrews before. During one of a series of matches between Young Tom Morris and Willie Park on April 12th, 1870, a huge throng of spectators followed the game. According to the umpire, a Colonel Dougall, "with the carrying of the rope behind the players, there had never been better order."

The maintenance staff of the R & A at St Andrews were mainly responsible for the presentation of the Old Course for the Championship but when one Overgreen conked out the Town Council workers from the Eden and Jubilee courses moved in to lend a hand. They brought in one of their own Overgreens and cut the greens in the late afternoon and evening, following the last players in as they headed for home. They took part too in setting up the fencing to carry the ropes. The men began at the first hole and took the posts all the way round the course except for the 17th where the rope was to be hand-held. Holes to anchor the posts were driven by an auger borrowed from a farmer and the 1.5 inch diameter rope was secured to each post by a half-hitch. To direct

LINKS WITH THE PAST

spectators over fairways, railway signal type poles were used. In the "up" position they read "Cross Here".

The passing into history of the "free-for-all" stampede did not go unmourned. Writing in Country Life in 1947 Bernard Darwin recognised the need for roping and went so far as to suggest that St Andrews was the ideal site for it but he continued: "In old unregenerate days of St Andrews, running was regarded as part of the fun and tradition, to be hilariously observed. The young ladies and gentlemen of the University were leaders of the revels. I have a vision of a swirling mass of scarlet gowns rampaging up the course towards the second hole while I proceed behind at a more leisurely pace, swearing gently to myself."

The first and 18th fairways of the Eden Course were set aside for car parking and this arrangement during the tournament almost brought disaster. A grass fire broke out by the side of the railway track and spread quickly towards the cars. Those in greatest danger were hastily pulled away by tractor and chain. The Fire Brigade put out the blaze.

Volunteers had helped construct a sloping ramp of sand behind the 17th green, an observation stance that was the forerunner of today's imposing grandstands.

Close by this ramp, in a railway siding, visitors from London and the south were to have a final day treat. Spaldings had organised a train special to the event. Included in the price were tickets for access to the course and lunch and dinner on board. The train arrived at 8 a.m. on the last day, its passengers helping to swell the crowd to a healthy 15,000.

Among the workforce preparing for the Open were about 15 German prisoners of war, who had helped form new pathways to ease the passage of the crowds. They were based at a POW camp at Lathockar about five miles away. The prisoners were frequent visitors to the rubbish tip that stretched out along the West Sands. They picked up any pieces of scrap metal they could find and from this unpromising material, crafted the most wonderful toys.

Another issue which might have affected the Open was discussed by the R & A at their spring meeting - the increasing clamour for the bigger golf ball, as played in the United States.

Concern was mounting over the great distances carried by the standard British ball and what was seen as the emasculation of certain courses but it was also stated that while the bigger ball might fly less far, it was easier to strike and control, except in wind. It was not heavier than the British ball, only bigger.

The R & A meeting was in response to a forum held in London during January, 1945, originated by the English Golf Union. The Union felt "the time had come" to restrict the performance of the golf ball. This echoes uncannily the same worry today but even then the problem was not a new one. There had been discussions on the issue since 1922 when the specifications of the British ball were improved.

During October 1917, the Dunlop Rubber Company, using a driving machine, tested their famous '29' and '31' balls against the balls of an unnamed commercial competitor. In a slight cross wind the '29' carried an average 630 feet from machine to pitch compared to 623 feet for the rival. The '31' carried 612 feet against 608. The competitor may well have been the Avon ball, launched as a cheaper alternative to the Dunlops. Retailing at one shilling and ninepence, it was ninepence cheaper than the '29'. Avon also produced a ball at one shilling and threepence, the Nova, which is simply Avon spelled backwards.

No action was taken by the R & A and the matter was shelved for at least three years, leaving it up to the players themselves which size of ball they used. Surprisingly perhaps, most Americans used the small ball while in Britain. It would be 1968 before the British P. G. A. ruled that only the larger ball was to be played in all tournaments.

Entry fees for the Open were fixed for residents of the town at two shillings and sixpence per day, with reductions for children. Visitors faced a daily charge of four shillings and sixpence.

Caddie rates were settled as follows: for practice rounds, seven shillings and sixpence per round; for the Open proper, ten shillings a round.

Sites on the links were rented out to traders to operate refreshment tents.

Accommodation in St Andrews itself was heavily booked, the major hotels charging between one and five guineas per day for full board. For your five guineas you got an entire suite. The Grand Hotel charged £2. 2s. per day, full board. Some hoteliers found themselves accused of over-charging during the Open week and the Provost of the town, George Bruce, went to bat on their behalf. Due largely to his intervention the storm died away almost as soon as it began. The East Neuk towns a few miles to the south were packed to the rafters with golf fans, most of whom commuted to the course by bus or train.

For the first time since the end of the war camping was allowed on the Kinkell Braes and many golfing enthusiasts gathered there. (During March, 1945, an application by a Boys Brigade unit to camp on the practice ground of the Eden Course in July that year had been approved by the Town Council, who hurriedly changed their minds following complaints from local golfers).

LINKS WITH THE PAST

On the course itself some tees had been moved back, others forward, the net result being a lengthening by 40 yards.

The war, like all wars, had produced prodigious strides in the development of technology and the 1946 Open was the first ever to make widespread use of the "walkie-talkie" radio system. Range of each of the four sets was about one mile. Another innovation was the 50-foot portable scoreboard, equipped with loudspeakers. This was seldom on the course. It usually stood 100 yards behind the R & A clubhouse, just east of the bandstand so that people not watching the play could be kept informed of the tournament's progress.

Television coverage was a long way into the future - the 1955 Open would be the first fully-televised event - and with Press reports severely edited on account of the paper shortage, BBC Radio ought to have had a field day with this, the first Open for seven years. Incredibly, the service delivered on air the broadcasting equivalent of an air shot and listeners had to make do with nominal coverage.

One person driving to compete in the Open was the amateur R. R. Kelly of the Royal Norwich Club. At York his car was involved in an accident and Kelly had to continue on by rail. On arrival at St Andrews on the Saturday morning Kelly said: "I have had two front teeth knocked out and the only trouble is I can't whistle."

That same day during practice Lawson Little's exuberance extended to a leap which cleared the Swilcan Burn. The American, who had served for three years aboard an aircraft carrier during the war, was destined to have the best aggregate over the last two rounds - but not to win. Saturday afternoon was a wash-out, the torrential rain preventing any practice rounds.

Everyone who turned up to play had to undergo qualification to gain one of the 100 places in the Open, even reigning champion Dick Burton, who had won at St Andrews in 1939. He had found that experience so draining that he had to be assisted off the last green.

The weeding-out took place on Monday and Tuesday, when Snead tackled his Old Course round wearing a yellow sweater and a grey cowboy hat. Although rounds of 75 and 74 qualified him with the greatest of ease it was apparent that Snead - then ranked six in America - had not yet overcome the putting problems which beset him during the U. S. Open that summer. Henry Cotton too, seemed ill at ease on the enormous greens. It may not have helped Cotton that he had become involved in something of a wrangle in the lead-up to the event, having suggested construction of a grandstand over the railway line at the 16th. His idea was turned down.

Snead, another U. S. Navy veteran, gave notice that his powerful game would be a factor in the Open when on the Monday he got within 10 feet of the flag at the long 8th on the New in two shots, the second being a three iron. At the same hole Locke, no mean hitter himself, was short in two with a driver and a brassie.

That same day Dick Burton had thrilled the galleries on the third of the Old when he almost holed his approach. Unfortunately the same player had to leave the 10th green rather red in the face having just taken four putts. But champions are made of stern stuff. He sank a 30-footer for birdie at the next.

Norman von Nida, from New South Wales, Australia, put in a solid performance despite wearing three sweaters and waterproofs as the breeze from a long-dead season passed over the links in a cold, measured gait.

The fiery greens were worrying everyone and Bulla delighted those of the 1,691 paying fans who saw him by a theatrical tremble as he prepared to putt.

Disaster struck an emerging Scottish talent, John Panton. The young assistant from Pitlochry had all unknowing, practised on forbidden greens before the preliminary rounds were completed. He reported his error to the tournament committee who had no option but to disqualify him. They made a point of stating that they "greatly appreciated his conduct."

Those players who qualified all scored 159 or better.

> It must seem incredible to the golf fan of today but normal play was permitted on both the Jubilee and New Courses while the Open was in progress at a cost per round of two shillings (New) and one shilling (Jubilee).

Day One of the Open dawned bright, warm and calm and proved much to the advantage of the early starters, among whom were Cotton and Locke.

Cotton's fine 70 included just 30 putts and was beaten only by Locke's stunning 69, which he described as his best round ever. Cotton's circumnavigation of the Old Course, a model of consistency, saw him reach every two-shot green in two from the first to the 14th, with the exception of the sixth where he pitched and single putted. Gone with the wind, it seemed, were the putting uncertainties of the qualifying rounds.

Also out in the morning von Nida had astonished everyone by turning up in an open-necked shirt. The conditions plainly suited him and he put together a flawless 70.

The later starters had to contend with a stiff easterly breeze which added a good three shots to the back nine. Even so, Bulla was four under fours standing on the 17th tee. The genial American's second shot, off a downhill lie, flew the

LINKS WITH THE PAST

green and alighted on the dreaded road. It took him three further strokes to get onto the putting surface and the resultant seven put an ugly blemish on his card. He finished in 71, as did Snead.

Among other scores that day were a 71 for Joe Kirkwood, 73 for Charlie Ward, 74 for Percy Alliss and 75 for Dai Rees. The little Welshman's unexceptional round gave no hint of what was to unfold the following day.

The golfers on Day Two found stormy conditions in the morning and among the most memorable rounds to emerge from that part of the day was that of the amateur Andrew Dowie, from the town of Cupar, 10 miles away. Severe overnight rain had softened the greens considerably and he putted like a demon for his 71, which must have gone a long way to erase the memory of a first-round 81. Dowie was destined to flounder over the last two rounds and after his 80 and 83 he admitted the greens had beaten him - a telling observation from someone who had tackled them hundreds of times.

Sam Snead's 71 looked like leading the Open after Round Two but in the final grouping Henry Cotton was still on the course. The Royal Mid Surrey golfer, out in 35, had started back well but spoiled the run with a half dozen at the 15th after pushing a six iron right of the green. Undismayed, Cotton launched his second to the 16th to 10 feet and holed for a birdie. Now two under fours he needed to finish in par figures to match Snead.

At the 17th, a par five then, Cotton had to execute the most delicate of chip shots over the greenside bunker and holed from six feet for par. At the 18th a concerted roar burst from the throats of the crowd as he rammed home a 10-yarder for a three and took the lead.

But if Cotton was on fire, Rees was positively molten.

Out in the early afternoon the Hindhead professional committed just one error in his round, taking five at the 13th where his second found a bunker. Watched by his father Rees took the Old Course apart for a 67, equalling Bill Nolan's record which had stood since 1933. His figures: OUT - 4, 4, 3, 4, 4, 4, 4, 3, 3. IN - 4, 3, 4, 5, 4, 4, 3, 4, 3.

He had "putted like an angel" and was now just two shots out of the lead. His dazed dad kept muttering: "67! 67!"

Alf Padgham had weathered the early conditions well and took 34 to the turn but in the inexplicable way of golf, rather faded along with the wind and ended with a 74. Padgham had had to render first aid to his playing partner's caddie who suffered a cut eye while ducking under a rope.

Lawson Little had told his caddie he was "going to shoot the works" and began well with 4, 3, 4, having lipped out for a birdie at the first. His inward nine however produced a spate of misfortunes, including an out-of-bounds at the 14th where he took seven and he completed the round in 75.

Percy Alliss found some form and despite missing many a makeable putt, was round in 72 and six shots back.

LINKS WITH THE PAST

On the same mark was von Nida whose drive at the 17th had been heading out of bounds when it cannoned off the stationmaster's cottage and back onto the fairway. (Before it became known as The Road Hole, the 17th had been called The Stationmaster's Garden). The Australian had not had a good day and subtracted from it with an angry exchange with a cameraman on the 17th green.

The Jigger Inn, formerly the Stationmaster's Cottage.

The 33-year-old Snead had continued to impress as the best of the American contingent and his 70 seemed almost effortless. Charlie Ward struck the top blow of the day, holing his tee shot at the 163-yard eighth. His single helped him to a 73. Locke was round in a steady 74.

Only 34 competitors survived to contest the final day, Friday, when two rounds were to be played. Among notable non-qualifiers were Max Faulkner, who would win the Open at Portrush in 1951, and Arthur Havers of Moor Park.

Thirty-six holes away from becoming the Open Champion - that was the Friday prospect for the players, six of whom were Scots. And might it have been the very proximity of that ultimate dream which compelled so many in that defining moment to succumb to the ancient angst which rubberises limbs, rots co-ordination and has so often reduced the genuinely gifted to the level of bare competence? Whatever the reason the golf proved to be unspectacular as not a single player bettered 72 in good scoring conditions.

Locke and Cotton both blew chances to win, their putters letting them down, notably on the inward half of the final round. Cotton's three putts on the home green, from five yards, told the story of his day and he finished with a miserable 79.

Locke shared second place with Bulla on 294 but how he must have rued the putts that got away! He hadn't been helped by the whirring of a cine camera on his backswing at the 10th tee in the morning and he cut the shot into a bunker.

LINKS WITH THE PAST

A camera then clicked at a vital moment on the 15th and he produced a horror hook - "My worst shot of the Championship" - to take five.

In what must surely bring a wry smile to the face of today's tour professional, one Press comment described Locke's third round of three hours as being played "at a snail's pace."

The South African's glowing tribute to the Old Course before the event was now stood on its head. He called for a complete re-design of the layout, incorporating parts of the New Course. Locke was to have another swipe at the Old Course in the lead-up to the 1955 Open when he astonished the golfing fraternity by referring to it as "un-natural." A considerably portlier Locke would return to play an unaltered Old Course in 1957 - and win. To no one's surprise the new Open Champion suddenly became a fan again, telling the onlookers in his victory address that the Open should always be played at St Andrews. Complimenting the workers who had prepared the course he said pre-tournament criticisms were "quite uncalled for."

Johnny Bulla must have suffered a feeling of deja-vous after completing the equal best round of the day, 72. He had been second in St Andrews in 1939.

Charlie Ward played the last day in 73 and 76, finishing with 295, while record-holder Rees had a reasonable 73 in the morning and a disastrous 80 after lunch, which perversely included a wonderful eagle at the 17th.

Rees had been full of confidence as he prepared to set out on his final round. However, his downswing on the 1st tee was interrupted by a loud shout from some Celtic clown. To the cry of Good Old Wales! Rees sliced his shot on this simplest of driving holes. Rank bad manners were followed by rank bad luck as his four-wood second just cleared the Swilcan Burn but rolled back into the water. A seven resulted and Rees never recovered.

It was to West Virginia that the Open title was destined to fly.

Sam Snead's success was the first in the tournament for an American since Densmore Shute's triumph in 1933 (The Shute Open was the first ever at which gate money was charged). And as Snead raised his hat when the final putt dropped, the crowd cheered a well-merited victory.

In the morning Snead had displayed all his prodigious power, "pouring the lumber" into his drive at the 422-yard sixth and getting close to the green. At the 316-yard 12th his tee shot did come to rest on the putting surface, then he proceeded to reduce the 546-yard 14th to a drive and a four iron. Crucially, he putted well.

The 10th green surrendered to his driver in three of the four rounds, minus any help from the wind.

Snead's moment of greatest danger came in the afternoon when he had two bad holes in a row - the fifth and sixth. He three-putted the fifth then contrived to land his drive at the next in Hell Bunker, a hazard designed for the 14th hole. From the sand he cut his ball over the ropes into the whins and made a hash of his recovery shot, finding a greenside bunker. In disgust, Snead threw his club against a fence post but recovered sufficient composure to get up and down. The hole had cost him a six but Slammin' Sam played confident golf from then on, his only other untidy hole coming at the 16th where he took five.

How often does it happen with the great champions? Snead immediately repaired the damage with a beautifully played 17th. Deliberately short in two he chipped up and holed for a birdie.

A solid par at the last gave him a winning margin of four clear strokes. It was noticed as he lined up his approach putt that a Stars and Stripes was fluttering boldly from the top of a nearby hotel. On the same building a Union Jack had somehow slipped to half-mast!

Snead with the famous Claret Jug

LINKS WITH THE PAST

The top dozen completed the tournament as follows:

S. J. Snead:	71, 70, 74, 75
A. D. Locke:	69, 74, 75, 76
J. Bulla:	71, 72, 72, 79
C. H. Ward:	73, 73, 73, 76
T. H. Cotton:	70, 70, 76, 79
D. J. Rees:	76, 67, 73, 80
N. von Nida:	70, 76, 74, 75
F. Daly:	77, 71, 76, 74
J. Kirkwood:	71, 75, 78, 74
L. Little:	78, 75, 72, 74
H. Bradshaw:	76, 75, 76, 73
R. Burton:	74, 76, 76, 76

Top amateur was Mr R. K. Bell of Accrington and District, with a total of 312. Andrew Dowie was second.

There existed a school of thought which felt that the qualifying rounds should be included in the overall score to decide the championship, the theory being that the player showing the greatest consistency over the week would emerge as the winner. Under this system Snead would still have won.

The presentation ceremony took place at 7 p.m. although at first the Champion could not be found. Snead was having a bath!

The famous claret jug was handed over by Lord Wardington, the new President of the P. G. A. As he made his ultimately gracious speech, explaining this was one of the happiest days of his life, Snead might have had cause to wince at the memory of a close shave both he and Bulla had had on the opening day. They were nowhere to be seen when at 10.42 they were called to play by the starter, "Jimmie" Alexander. Fully three minutes elapsed before the pair sprinted onto the tee with a few seconds to spare before disqualification.

Old Course Starter "Jimmie" Alexander, affectionately referred to by local players as a "genial despot"

LINKS WITH THE PAST

In his address Snead said he thought it would be his day when on the third fairway a bird started singing away above his head. He looked forward to meeting the British stars again in the Ryder Cup - to be held in Britain wasn't it? - the following year. (It seems reasonable to put Snead's apparent uncertainty about the venue down to a tongue-in-cheek remark, although interest in the Ryder Cup was nowhere near as intense then as it is today. The Cup was duly played for in the United States at Portland, Oregon, in 1947).

Replying for the British players Henry Cotton ventured the view that they had all been so hungry that they just faded away. Most of the crowd would have been unaware of Cotton's ill health during the final years of the war in the Royal Air Force, nor of his operation and year-long convalescence in 1945/46.

He said: "We did not have the stomach to finish the course. I hope we will be able to win back the Ryder Cup when we get some good steaks!"

It was a fond hope. The British team undertook the long journey to the far coast of America only to suffer an embarrassing rout, 11 points to one. The humiliation seemed all the worse because most of the expenses of the trip had been paid for by an American businessman.

Cotton was able to put some of his disappointment behind him after the Open when two weeks later he won the French Open at St Cloud by a prodigious 15 strokes. His 70, 66, 67, 66 was a record score for the event.

Willie Auchterlonie who was consultant for the redesigned Jubilee Course completed in 1946

Among those listening to the closing speeches were Jack White, the Open Champion of 1904 and 1893 Champion Willie Auchterlonie, who had stewarded the 18th green throughout the tournament.

So ended the Open Championship of 1946. Not the most dramatic there has ever been but a feast of sport in an age so badly in need of it.

And what of the Champion?

Having won the Open at his first attempt Snead was heading straight for another tournament in Kansas City, via New York. As he prepared to board the Pan Am Clipper in London on Tuesday, July 9th, he told reporters:

"Every time I play in an American tournament, it is worth $500 to me as British Champion."

Snead did not venture to Hoylake the following year to defend his title.

Nevertheless when a semi-retired Byron Nelson arrived to compete in the 1955 Open, it was the words of Sam Snead he had ringing in his ears: "You've never played a real course until you've played the Old Course at St Andrews."

LINKS WITH THE PAST

In casting about for a last word with which to put a tidy end to this chapter the thought came to me that I had already found it. In all the world of golf, the Open IS the last word.

The question of charging the municipal voters of St Andrews green fees first raised its head in a serious way during 1945 and in an election address by Provost Bruce late that year he said "the time was coming" when locals would have to pay for golf.

Bruce was duly re-elected on polling day, November 6th, and after a meeting with the R & A on December 14th it was decided to recommend the promotion of a Provisional Order to permit the levying of charges upon locals.

The January 1946 meeting of the Town Council, although it did not know it at the time, conferred historical status upon Mr David Johnston of 2 Abbey Street and his wife and four children by approving the family's application for free golf. They were the last people ever to be accorded this ancient right.

The matter of the Provisional Order was raised formally at the monthly meeting of the Town Council on February 4th. The members voted without exception to back the Order for introducing fees for townspeople, the level to be decided later.

The Order, which was to cost £500 to administer, also specified among other matters that power would be granted to the Town Council to contribute towards the expenditures undertaken by the R & A for the upkeep of the Old and New courses (The club had asked for this help, having found the burden of maintenance increasingly severe).

The sum of £1,900 from the local authority towards the wartime upkeep of the courses was advanced as another reason for bringing in green fees, as was the cost of the re-design of the Jubilee Course, which was due to open for play on June 1st, 1946. Main consultant for this project had been local professional Willie Auchterlonie, with periodic input from the Board of Greenkeeping Research at Bingley, Yorkshire.

As the year advanced, so the level of protest from residents grew.

Provost Bruce, while outlining the Council's proposals at a meeting of the Ratepayers Association on Friday, May 3rd, was loudly heckled.

St Andrews Golf Club lodged an official complaint, citing a declaration by the Town Council in 1912 that the residents of St Andrews had "an inherent right" to free golf. If it was inherent then they argued, it was inherent now.

The Ratepayers Association was at times withering in its condemnation of the Town Council and such was the interest generated by the proposal - which would require an Act of Parliament to be passed - that the Secretary of State for Scotland decided to allow a public inquiry, to begin on Friday, July 26th. It was to last two days.

One misconception was advanced on many occasions throughout the period in support of the residents. It was their "birthright" to have free golf many declared but the 1894 Act of Parliament relating to the issue had stated that the citizens would be granted this privilege "by right of residence."

It was this Act which had permitted the Town Council to buy the links land from the R & A for £5,000, the same sum paid by the club to the previous owner, Mr James Cheape of Strathtyrum. The Town Council thereby regained ownership of the land, sold for about £800 by their profligate and inefficient predecessors in 1797 at a time when the town had lost most of its former influence and had become little more than a noisesome backwater. The R & A, by the 1894 statute, accepted responsibility to maintain the Old Course and to complete work on the New, then under construction at an estimated cost to the club of £2,000, thus giving St Andrews its second golf course. (The New, although never exclusive to R & A members, did have certain privileges built in for them and it generated income which WAS exclusive to the club. Today's club members continue to enjoy preferential tee times on the New Course).

The St Andrews Bill, as the legislation was known, passed ownership of the land to the Town Council. Negotiations between the Council and the club which preceded the passing of the Act had recognised the need "to safeguard these beautiful links from intrusion by any objectionable person."

The Town Council meeting of May, 1894 noted "the generous manner" in which the R & A had agreed to fund the New Course and maintain the Old, so enabling the Council to offer free golf to all - including visitors - on the Old all year round and on the New for nine months. The three main summer months were to be devoted to golf for R & A members and for local club players and residents only.

Management of the links for the purposes of golf were placed in the hands of a Green Committee consisting of five club members and two Town Councillors. These were agreed as Provost John McGregor and Baillie George Murray, both golfers, whose places on the Committee were to last out the 19th century as the game continued to be played with clubs carrying such evocative names as bulger and lofter.

The issue of the town's acquisition of the links prompted responses every whit as bitter as in 1946 and petitions against the move were lodged in Parliament.

A meeting held by opponents of the purchase in the Volunteer Hall on Monday, February 19th, 1894 ended in uproar, with applause and hissing and hooting greeting every speaker to varying degrees. Dr Hay Fleming spoke so eloquently in favour of the purchase that he left the platform with the strains of "For He's A Jolly Good Fellow" ringing in his ears.

LINKS WITH THE PAST

The matter was settled by the passing of the Act in April and a celebratory banquet was held by the victors in the Cross Keys Hotel on Thursday, August 2nd at 7 p.m.

Supporters of the 1946 Order pointed out that residents included lodgers who paid no rates and thus got genuinely free golf while the town's ratepayers actually paid fees already through an element added to their rates. It was also reiterated that, contrary to popular belief, there were far more non-golfers than golfers living in St Andrews and those upon whom rates were levied effectively paid an annual subscription for golf while owning not so much as a tee peg. In all the world of golf it is difficult to imagine a more bizarre arrangement.

The advocates of change finally won the day and the Order began to grind its way slowly through the parliamentary process. It achieved Royal Assent on December 19th but it was not until the Town Council met on Monday, March 3rd, 1947 that an annual fee of £1 was decided upon for local golfers, after consultation with local clubs.

A nominal sum it may have been but it proved to be the wafer-thin end of a wedge which has thickened over the years to the point where local golfers are paying about £100 as an annual fee to cover play on all St Andrews courses.

To bring to a suitable conclusion this visitation to the Home of Golf the end of a poem may serve as well as anything else. A collection of poetry - Golfiana - was written by a Scottish wordsmith who was born and raised in an area known as Angus and The Mearns. Fittingly, this is one of the great golfing centres of the world and home to the Championship Course at Carnoustie, widely held to be the toughest of all the Open Championship venues. The work by George Fullarton Carnegie (1799-1851) was completed in 1833, just one year after the course at St Andrews was redesigned to feature 18 brand-new holes. It strides off the final green with the following lines:

AND STILL ST. ANDREWS LINKS
WITH FLAGS UNFURL'D
SHALL PEERLESS REIGN
AND CHALLENGE ALL THE WORLD

BIBLIOGRAPHY AND SOURCE NOTES

1. St Andrews Town Council Minutes, 1894, 1897, 1939, 1940, 1941, 1942, 1943, 1944, 1945, 1946, 1947, 1953, 1954, 1955, 1974.

2. The St Andrews Opens: Bobby Burnett.

3. The St Andrews Citizen, May 21st, 1887; May 28th, 1887; January 3rd, 1914; July 11th, 1914; September 1st, 1917; July 6th and 13th, 1946; August 31st, 1946; March 11th, 1950; February 20th, 1957.

4. The Courier & Advertiser, April 30th, 1915; July 4th, 5th and 6th, 1946.

5. The Evening Telegraph, July 2nd, 3rd, 4th, 5th, 6th and 9th, 1946.

6. Golf Monthly, April and August issues, 1946.

7. The Encyclopaedia Britannica 11th Edition, Vol. X11, 1910.

8. "Illustrated" magazine, September, 1949.

9. The Fifeshire Journal, October 10th, 1867; January 2nd, 1868; March 24th, 1870; April 14th, 1870; May 19th, 1870; September 7th, 1871; August 29th, 1872; April 17th, 1879.

10. Pin High magazine, December, 1969.

11. Golfing Annual (Second Edition) 1894.

12. Golfiana - George Fullarton Carnegie, 1833.